M000285510

THE NORSE MYTHS

THE
NORSE MYTHS
A GUIDE TO THE
GODS AND HEROES

~~~~~~~~~~~~~~~~~

CAROLYNE LARRINGTON

WITH 102 ILLUSTRATIONS

For JJ, JQ, LA and HO'D

Page 1: Berserker warrior, from the Lewis Chessmen.
Frontispiece: The wolf Fenrir swallows Óðinn, from
the Viking-Age Thorwald Cross, Isle of Man.

First published in the United Kingdom in 2017 by
Thames & Hudson Ltd, 181A High Holborn,
London WC1V 7QX

First published in 2017 in hardcover in the
United States of America by Thames & Hudson Inc.,
500 Fifth Avenue, New York, New York 10110

Reprinted 2021

The Norse Myths © 2017 Thames & Hudson Ltd, London

All Rights Reserved. No part of this publication may
be reproduced or transmitted in any form or by any
means, electronic or mechanical, including photocopy,
recording or any other information storage and
retrieval system, without prior permission in writing
from the publisher.

British Library Cataloguing-in-Publication Data
A catalogue record for this book is available from
the British Library

Library of Congress Control Number 2016941839

ISBN 978-0-500-25196-6

Printed and bound in China by Toppan Leefung
Printing Limited

Be the first to know about our new releases,
exclusive content and author events by visiting
thamesandhudson.com
thamesandhudsonusa.com
thamesandhudson.com.au

CONTENTS

Old Norse names are cited in their Old Norse forms. This requires two unfamiliar letters (still used in modern Icelandic and Faroese), called 'eth' (ð / Ð) and 'thorn' (þ / Þ). The first of these is pronounced as the 'th' sound in 'the', for example in the name of the king of the gods, Óðinn (Odin). The second is pronounced as the 'th' sound in 'thorn', as in the name of Þórr (Thor).

Scholars usually pronounce Old Norse words as if they were modern Icelandic. Stress falls on the first syllable. Most consonants are pronounced as in English (with 'g' always hard as in 'gate', but 'j' pronounced as 'y' as in 'yes'). So: 'Gerðr' = 'GAIR-ther' (the capitals show the stress).

Vowels are also pronounced as in English when short, though short 'a' is like 'a' of 'father', not as in 'cat'. 'y' is the same as 'i': 'Gylfi' = 'GIL-vee'. 'll' is pronounced like 'tl': Valhöll = VAL-hertl.

Long vowels (marked with an acute accent) are mostly just a longer version of the short ones, though 'á' is like 'ow' as in 'how'. The goddesses are collectively called the Ásynjur = 'OW-sin-yur'.

Diphthongs are somewhat different: 'ei' or 'ey' is 'ay', as in 'hay', so Freyr = 'FRAY-er; 'au' is a little like 'oh', but longer than in English. 'draumar' (dreams) = DROH-mar.

'æ' is pronounced 'eye', so the 'Æsir' (the main group of gods) = 'EYE-seer'.

'ö' and 'ø' are like German 'ö': something like 'er'. Thus 'Jötunheimar' (the lands of the giants) = 'YER-tun-HAY-mar'.

I would like to thank Tim Bourns for many useful suggestions and for his work on the index. The four dedicatees have been instigators of, and companions on, many Norse adventures in many lands: *til góðs vínar liggja gagnvegir, þótt hann sé firr farinn.*

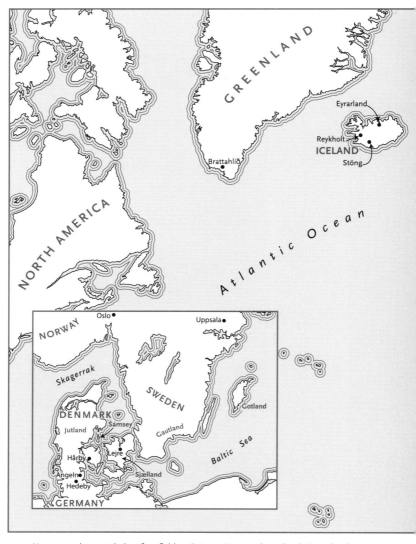

Norse-speakers settled as far afield as Britain, Normandy, Iceland, Greenland and North America. They settled in Russia, and worked in Constantinople as the emperor's Varangian Guard.

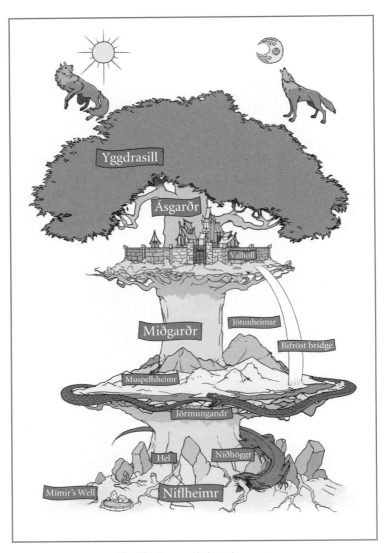

The Old Norse mythological cosmos.

Óðinn [Odin] was a man remarkable for his wisdom and in all
accomplishments. His wife was called Frigida, and we call her Frigg.
Óðinn had prophetic abilities and so did his wife, and from this
knowledge he discovered that he would become extremely famous
in the northern part of the world, and honoured above all kings.
For this reason he was eager to journey away from Turkey, and he
brought a great multitude of people with him, young and old, men
and women, and they brought many precious things with them.
But wherever they went in the continent, so many splendid things
were said of them that they seemed more like gods than men.

SNORRI STURLUSON, PROLOGUE, *Prose Edda* (*c.* 1230)

⚔ SNORRI STURLUSON AND THE CLEVER ASIAN MIGRANTS ⚔

Who were the Norse gods? Migrants from the Near East, journeying up through Germany to reach the promised Scandinavian
homeland: humans like you and me, but smarter, handsomer, more
civilized. Or so claimed one Christian writer, a medieval Icelander
who recorded many of the myths and legends that have survived
from the Scandinavian north. Medieval Christian scholars needed
to explain why their ancestors worshipped false gods, and thus one
widespread theory was that the pre-Christian gods were demons,
wicked spirits sent by Satan to tempt humans into sin and error.
But another very effective theory was the one put forward by Snorri
Sturluson in the quotation above: the so-called gods were in fact
exceptional humans, immigrants from Troy, an idea known as
euhemerism. For Snorri Sturluson, the thirteenth-century Icelandic
scholar, politician, poet and chieftain who left us the most complete
and systematic account of the Norse pantheon, the idea that the

Norse gods – the Æsir as they were called – must have been human beings was compelling. Descendants of the losing side in the Trojan War, they decided to migrate northwards, bringing their superior technology and wisdom to the natives of Germany and Scandinavia. The incomers' culture overwhelmed that of the earlier inhabitants, who adopted the language of the new arrivals, and, after the death of the first immigrant generation, began to worship them as gods.

Snorri's explanation of how traditional Norse poetry worked in his *Edda* required a good deal of mythological background information, and so he created a framework that made clear that while no one *now* might worship the pagan gods – who were, anyway, nothing but a cunning tribe of Near Eastern migrants – the stories associated with them were both meaningful and entertaining. He therefore prefaced his treatise on poetics with a tale about King Gylfi of Sweden who was doubly beguiled; first by the goddess Gefjun, as related in Chapter 1, and a second time when Gylfi realized too late that he'd been tricked and set out for Ásgarðr, where he knew the Æsir lived. Gylfi intended to find out more about these deceivers; he was admitted to the king's hall and there he met three figures called Hár, Jafnhár and Þriði (High, Just-as-High and Third).

The Icelandic Scholar, Snorri Sturluson

Snorri Sturluson (1179–1241) belonged to a prominent Icelandic family and was deeply involved in the turbulent politics of Iceland and of Norway. He composed a treatise on poetics, known as the *Prose Edda*, which consists of four parts: a long poem illustrating various kinds of poetic metres called *Háttatal* (List of Metres); *Skáldskaparmál* (The Language of Poetry), an explanation of the metaphorical figures known as kennings (see page 15); a *Prologue*; and a section known as *Gylfaginning* (The Tricking of Gylfi). Snorri was murdered in a cellar at his home in Reykholt in Iceland by agents acting for the Norwegian king: his last words were, 'Don't strike!'

Statue of Snorri Sturluson, the thirteenth-century Icelandic scholar, politician and poet, at his home at Reykholt, Iceland.

In a long question-and-answer session, Gylfi discovered a great deal about the gods, about the processes of the creation of the universe and of humanity, about the end of the world, *ragnarök*, in which the gods and giants would battle one another, and finally how the earth would be made anew. And, advising Gylfi to make good use of what he had heard, Hár and his two colleagues, the mighty hall and the imposing fortress, all vanished. Gylfi returned home to relay to others what he'd learned.

Snorri wrote a second important account of the Norse gods: *Ynglinga saga* (The Saga of the Ynglings), the first part of his history of the kings of Norway, known from its opening words as

King Gylfi meets Hár, Jafnhár and Þriði, from an eighteenth-century Icelandic manuscript.

Heimskringla (The Disc of the World). Here he adopted the same euhemeristic explanation of the Æsir as he put forward in his *Edda*, but he added further details about their capabilities and made clear that they were the ancestors of the kings of both Sweden and Norway. Snorri's mythological writings, rationalizing and systematizing though they are, give us crucial insight into narratives of the Norse gods and heroes. However, when reading Snorri's works, we need to bear in mind always that he writes as a medieval Christian and shapes some of his material accordingly. Thus he introduces the idea of a primeval flood which drowns all but one of the frost-giants, an invention driven by the biblical Noah's flood and the annihilation of the giants there. There's no evidence for this story anywhere else in surviving Norse tradition. Although Snorri must have known quite a lot more about Norse myth than we do, sometimes he comes across concepts that he does not fully understand,

and then he makes things up. We suspect too that Snorri knows of more stories than he relates – perhaps Óðinn's sacrifice of 'himself to himself' on the great World-Tree Yggdrasill (see Chapter 1). This myth of the hanged sacrificial god probably clashed too uncomfortably with the story of Christ's Crucifixion for a good Christian to be happy about recounting it.

⚜ TWO KINDS OF NORSE POETRY ⚜

No one is sure exactly what the word *edda* signifies; the name is given to Snorri's treatise in one of its earliest manuscripts. One meaning is 'great-grandmother'; this may point to the idea of mythological knowledge as ancient and closely associated with women. In fourteenth-century Iceland the word was used to mean something like 'poetics'. Old Norse poetry comes in two varieties. One kind is highly wrought: known as skaldic poetry, it employs a riddling metaphorical system known as the *kenning*. In their simplest form, kennings may be compounds, such as 'thought-smith' for 'poet' or 'elf-ray' for 'sun'. Many kennings, however, are more complex and riddling; they depend upon knowledge of mythology for their decipherment. Thus, in order to understand who the *farmr arma Gunnlaðar* (burden of Gunnlöð's arms) must be, we need to know that the god Óðinn once had occasion to seduce Gunnlöð, a giant's daughter, in order to win the mead of poetry for gods and men (see Chapter 3). Describing Óðinn in these terms instead of, for example, 'the hanged god', sets up associations with the god as seducer, one who obtains culturally vital treasures for gods and men, rather than as the suffering figure who hangs himself on the World-Tree in order to win knowledge of the runes; sacrifice by hanging seems to be the best way of pleasing Óðinn. A very few mythological narratives, notably some adventures of Þórr (Thor) discussed in Chapter 3, are recorded in skaldic verse, but the main

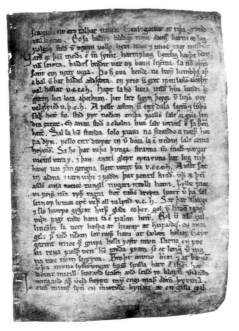

The Codex Regius manuscript, from *c.* 1270, showing some verses from *Völuspá* (The Seeress's Prophecy).

relevance of myth and legend to this kind of poetry is that they underpin the metaphors of the kenning system.

The second kind of Old Norse poetry is called eddic poetry, and it shares its simpler alliterative form with the early verse composed in the related Germanic languages of Old English and Old High German. The term 'eddic' was applied to this form of poetry because many of the stories that it retells formed the basis of Snorri's mythological account in his *Edda*. Much of the surviving poetry in this metre is preserved in a single manuscript, known officially as GKS 2365 4to, kept today in the Manuscript Institute in Reykjavík, the Stofnun Árna Magnússonar. An Icelandic bishop, Brynjólfur Sveinsson, presented this manuscript to the king of Denmark in

1662, and thus it has come to be known as the Codex Regius, the King's Codex. Although the codex was written in Iceland around 1270, many of the poems and much of the information in it were already known to Snorri, writing forty or so years earlier. It seems likely that there were some pre-existing written collections of mythological and heroic poetry that Snorri drew upon. Almost all the poems quoted in this book are from this compilation, but there are a few other mythological eddic poems beyond those found in the Codex Regius. These include *Baldrs Draumar* (Baldr's Dreams), foreshadowing the god Baldr's death, *Hyndluljóð* (Hyndla's Song), a poem that imparts lots of mythological information as a giantess lists the ancestors of one of the goddess Freyja's favourite heroes, and *Rígsþula* (Rígr's List), which relates how the social classes came into existence. Other eddic-style poems, many relating stories of ancient Scandinavian heroes, are to be found in prose tales (sagas) of Viking-Age heroes; these are known as *fornaldarsögur* (sagas of ancient times).

☒ SAXO: THE FIRST DANISH HISTORIAN ☒

Almost all the medieval accounts of Old Norse myth and legend originated in Iceland and in Icelandic. An important exception, however, is the *History of the Danes*, a massive account written in Latin by the Danish monk Saxo Grammaticus, who lived from around 1150 to 1220. Saxo's nickname means 'the learned'. In his Preface, Saxo tells us that, in the pre-Christian past, the Danes had 'engraved the letters of their own language on rocks and stones to retell those feats of their ancestors which had been made popular in the songs of their mother tongue'. Saxo also mentions that contemporary Icelanders were excellent sources of traditional tales, and he uses their material for his book. Like Snorri, Saxo characterizes the gods and heroes whose stories he relates as humans, often ingenious

A reconstructed medieval farm at Stöng in southern Iceland.

Tales Told in Iceland

Saxo's claims about how Icelanders remembered and preserved heroic tradition are borne out by the fact that our two major sources for Norse myth and legend, the *Prose* and *Poetic Eddas*, were indeed written down on the North Atlantic island. Iceland was settled largely from Norway in the ninth century. The origin myth of the Icelanders claims that they were descended from free-born nobles who would not accept the tyranny of King Haraldr Fair-hair, so they emigrated. Other Scandinavians from the Anglo–Scandinavian colonies of the British Isles moved to the new settlement, and slaves were imported from Celtic regions. Ancient stories from the Scandinavian homelands must also have travelled to Iceland on the settlers' longboats, to be recalled and performed in the little turf-roofed farmhouses where the households hunkered down during the long, dark winter nights, and so Iceland became, for centuries, the repository of knowledge about the pagan past.

and treacherous, who lived in Denmark's prehistoric past. Óðinn is once again said to be an extremely clever human being, 'a man ... widely believed throughout Europe, though falsely, to be a god'. Despite Saxo's sceptical tone, he records a great deal that supports the tales related elsewhere; he is particularly useful in giving further information on some of the more important Scandinavian heroes: Starkaðr and Ragnarr loðbrók (Shaggy-breeches), for example, whose stories are told in Chapter 5.

⚜ THE ORAL AND LITERARY ⚜

Snorri may very well have had little manuscript collections of eddic poetry at his elbow when he was composing his *Prose Edda*. But it is easy to underestimate the enormous amount of material that medieval people could store in their memories. Snorri's mind was no doubt stocked with a huge number of poems, both skaldic and eddic. From these works, and perhaps from prose retellings too, he drew the information that he needed to write his *Edda*. Snorri's writing would, in effect, fix the forms of Old Norse myths for future generations – an inevitable outcome when protean, variable stories are locked up in written form. But there never is, and never was, an 'original' version of a myth; it's impossible to establish who told the story first. Each individual retelling contributes to our overall understanding of the myth's structure and meaning. Each new version offers insight into mythic thinking and the contexts which make that myth relevant to the cultures that make use of it, whether in a whole poem, or a kenning, or an allusion, or in visual depictions on stone or wood carvings, or in paintings, textiles or ceramics.

As we'll see in Chapter 2, there's more than one explanation for the creation of the world in Norse myth, but there is nothing to be gained from arguing that one or another is the 'real' or 'original' story. Just as versions of Egyptian myths vary considerably along the whole length of the River Nile, so the Old Norse myths were the cultural property of all Viking-descended folk, wherever they lived across the northern world. In what's been called the Viking

Riders, ships, and stylized trees on a Viking-Age tapestry
from Överhogdal in Sweden.

diaspora, Norse-speaking people emigrated from Scandinavia to parts of Britain and to Normandy, to the North Atlantic islands – to Iceland primarily, but also to the Faroes, Orkney and Shetland. Later they would colonize southern Greenland and even establish short-lived settlements in North America. Scandinavians sailed down the Dnieper River to the Black Sea and gained employment as the Emperor's Varangian Guard in Constantinople, and they also founded the first Russian principalities.

This geographical dispersion meant that there could be no uniformity, no dogmatic version of the myths which everyone had to accept. Dogma is, by and large, associated with religions of the Book: Judaism, Christianity and Islam, faiths in which the sacred writings evolve, become accepted as canonical and then harden into orthodoxy (even if there are differences of interpretation). Ranging from the Jutland peninsula in Denmark, north to the borders of Lapland, west as far as Viking-Age Dublin and even Greenland, south to Normandy, and east to Constantinople, each Norse-speaking community knew and used a varying set of myths to explain the big metaphysical questions which it is myth's task to answer.

Legends change as they migrate across territorial and language boundaries. If we compare the version of the Sigurðr/Siegfried story preserved in the Austrian–German *Nibelungenlied* from around 1200, and the Norse poetic and prose versions, retold in Chapter 4, we find that the relationships between the main characters are completely reoriented. In the southern version, the main focus is on a sister's revenge on her brothers for slaying her husband. In the northern versions, the sister forgives her brothers and takes terrible vengeance on her second husband for murdering them. These variations tell us something about changing cultural norms; the stories explore where a sister's true loyalty might lie once she has become a wife. Myths and legends are mutable, labile; if they have a cultural role they are remembered, reshaped and, usually through writing or other forms of fixing, preserved. If they no longer hold meaning, they vanish. There must have been a huge number of stories of gods and heroes that did not make it into the Norse 'myth-kitty', tales of local or culture-wide currency that are now lost for ever.

❧ PLACES AND OBJECTS ❧

Some clues about the lost treasure of the 'myth-kitty' are offered by early references to pre-Christian religion, by archaeological finds or – particularly important in the Old Norse cultural area – by stone sculpture. Although much Old Norse religious ritual seems to have taken place outdoors, temples were built. There's an account dating from the 1070s, written by a scholar named Adam of Bremen, of the great temple at Uppsala in central Sweden. Sweden converted to Christianity rather later than Norway and Iceland, and Uppsala was a centre for all kinds of activities: political, administrative, religious and legal. Statues of Thor, Wotan and Frikko (Þórr, Óðinn and Freyr) were enthroned in the Uppsala temple, Adam tells us. Þórr occupied the central position while the other two gods sat on either side. Near the temple was a huge evergreen tree, with a well beneath it in which men were drowned as offerings. Both humans and animals were sacrificed by hanging on the tree, dogs, horses and

Depiction of the great temple at Uppsala, with a sacrificed man visible in the well, from *A Description of the Northern Peoples* by Olaus Magnus (1555).

The Oseberg Ship-Burial

In 1903 a farmer in Vestfold, southern Norway, discovered part of a ship when digging into a mound in his fields. Archaeologists from the University of Oslo excavated the site the following summer and uncovered a huge, richly carved ship, 21.5 metres (70 feet 6 inches) long and 5 metres (16 feet 5 inches) wide. The ship had been manufactured from oak timber around 820 CE, and it was capable of being rowed by thirty oarsmen. The ship had been dragged up onto the land in 834 CE and used for the tomb of two obviously high-status women. One was aged between seventy and eighty, the other probably around fifty, and they lay together on a bed in a splendidly decorated hut erected behind the ship's mast. The burial chamber was hung with ornate tapestries, and contained lots of possessions: furniture, clothing, shoes, combs, sledges and an elaborately decorated bucket were all arranged around the women. The skeletons of fifteen horses, six dogs and two small cows were also present. The mound was broken into during the medieval past and all the precious metal objects which must have been buried there were stolen, but the high quality of the larger and heavier items that remained suggest that the older woman might well have been a queen. You can see the Oseberg ship, and two others like it, at the Viking Ship Museum in Oslo.

men all dangling together. As mentioned above, myths associated with Óðinn emphasize the importance of hanging as the primary form of sacrificial death.

Archaeological finds also buttress our understanding of the Norse mythic world, giving us a sense of what the weapons, shields, houses and boats mentioned in the stories might have looked like. Such material objects expand our imaginative recreation of the worlds of gods and heroes. Some items found in graves suggest that certain men and women were magic-practitioners who used mysterious objects in their rituals. Descriptions of ship-burials in mythic texts indicate that funeral vessels were set ablaze or sent out to sea;. This kind of ceremony would not leave any archaeological traces; nevertheless, the Oseberg ship-burial proves that ships were indeed thought appropriate for entombing the bodies of high-born men and women.

The ninth-century Oseberg ship, on display at the Viking Ship Museum in Oslo, Norway.

An Early Gotlandic Picture-Stone

One striking picture-stone image comes from Austers in the parish of Hangvar on Gotland and dates from between 400 and 600 CE. It shows a multi-legged monster with a human figure perhaps placing its hand in the beast's mouth, or at least seizing its lower jaw. This scene has been compared with the story of Týr who lost his hand to the cosmic wolf Fenrir, but it takes some imagination to see this strange millipede-like creature as a representation of the beast that will swallow up Óðinn at the end of the world.

The picture-stone from Austers in Hangvar, Gotland.

Most important for confirming and elaborating the myths and legends of the north are the Viking-Age stone sculptures – incised picture-stones or carved three-dimensional representations of supernatural or heroic figures. These are chiefly preserved in island outposts of the Viking diaspora, such as the Isle of Man or the island of Gotland, lying in the Baltic Sea between Sweden and Finland, which has long been a crossroads for trade and travel in the northern seas. Gotland has 475 surviving picture-stones with carved representations of complex scenes. The idiosyncratic details have made it possible to identify Óðinn on his eight-legged horse Sleipnir (see Chapter 1), scenes from the legend of Völundr the smith (see Chapter 2), and parts of the Sigurðr legend (Chapter 4).

Sometimes, as with Óðinn's eight-legged horse or the representations of the god Þórr fishing for the Miðgarðs-serpent with his ox-head bait, there's a detail so particular that it can only be explained as belonging to a particular Norse myth. Thus we can connect surviving myths and legends with stone sculptures across the Viking world. In each community, local tradition fused with inherited story, nowhere more strikingly than in the Isle of Man

Þórr and the giant Hymir fishing with an ox-head for bait (Chapter 3), on the (probably) tenth-century Gosforth fishing-stone from Cumbria, northern England.

where Norse legendary images were carved onto Christian crosses, setting up dialogues with Christian belief. Motifs from the story of Sigurðr the Dragon-Slayer could recall the battle of St Michael and the Dragon in the Book of Revelation. Óðinn's death, swallowed by the wolf Fenrir at *ragnarök*, is depicted on a cross-shaft known as Thorwald's Cross (after its carver who signs his name in runes) from Kirk Andreas in Man (see frontispiece). The image offers a powerful contrast to Christ who, unlike the All-father, will rise again after his death. Sigurðr's story is depicted also on stones and objects from as far afield as the Volga region of Russia and the famous Ramsund stone in Sweden (see page 140). We'll see in later chapters how these images mesh with the textual sources.

Increasingly, new metalwork finds, often of very tiny figures, are being identified as images of the Norse gods. These include a recently unearthed representation of Óðinn from Lejre in Denmark, enthroned with his two ravens perched on his chairback, and a stunning example of an armed female figure (a valkyrie) excavated at Hårby in Denmark. These take their places besides the

'Óðinn' from Lejre in Denmark. The figure is flanked by two ravens, and wears female costume.

Left: A female figure with sword and shield, possibly a valkyrie, *c.* 800.
Recently excavated at Hårby, Denmark. Right: A small metal figure
thought to be Freyr, from Rällinge, Sweden.

well-known image of Þórr from Eyrarland in Iceland (see page 103)
and the little statue with the huge phallus from Rällinge, Sweden,
usually identified as Freyr. The interplay between archaeology, myth
and legend is a dynamic one; new discoveries continue to inflect
and reconfigure our imaginative understanding.

☒ OTHER GERMANIC TRADITIONS ☒

Finally, in interpreting Norse myths we can make use of compara-
tive traditions from the early medieval Germanic-speaking world.
The Anglo-Saxons worshipped gods with similar names to those of
the Old Norse gods – Tiw, Woden, Thunor, Fricg, who give their
names to the days of the week (Tuesday, Wednesday, Thursday and
Friday), as do Týr, Óðinn, Þórr and Frigg in the Scandinavian languages. There are very few references to the gods in Old English
literature; one occurs in wisdom poetry, where Christ's saving

powers are contrasted with the contention that *Woden worhte weos* (Woden made idols). Another is found in the 'Nine Herbs Charm' which invokes Woden as striking a serpent with nine *wuldortanas* (glory-twigs). Among the slim number of texts surviving in Old High German are some charms, mentioning gods with recognizably similar names to those of the Old Norse pantheon.

In comparison with the rich explanations of Snorri's *Prose Edda* or even the logic of the tales in eddic poetry, these fragments from neighbouring cultures are provokingly mysterious. The Anglo-Saxon Church had no interest in preserving pre-Christian beliefs and its long monopoly over writing meant a wholesale loss of the story-hoard of the pagan past. Nor was mythic material saved from oblivion in the continental German homelands of the Anglo-Saxons, where English missionaries were in the business of saving souls and destroying pagan sanctuaries. Heroic legend survived a little better in both languages, and we'll have recourse to the Old English epic *Beowulf*, and the poem *Deor*, along with the German *Nibelungenlied*, to illuminate the heroic legends of Scandinavia along our way.

1

~~~~~~

THE GODS
AND GODDESSES

There are two distinct groups of Norse gods, the majority Æsir and the altogether more mysterious Vanir. Both tribes have male and female members, but although the female Æsir are known as Ásynjur (goddesses), the Vanir don't seem to have a separate term for their females, perhaps because Freyja is the only one we know about. *Æsir* is the plural of the noun *Áss*, meaning 'god'; when the term is used by itself as 'the Áss', it usually refers to Þórr.

⚔ THE ÆSIR ⚔

Óðinn, whose name means something like 'the Furious One', is the leader of the gods; he is sometimes called the 'All-father', but it is not a name that crops up often. He's a war-god, but unlike Freyr,

---

Óðinn
- Leader of the Æsir. One-eyed, bearded, old.
- God of wisdom, magic, battle, kingship; worshipped by the elite; chooser of the slain.
- Attribute: spear called Gungnir.
- Halls: chiefly Valhöll (Valhalla, Hall of the Slain), but a number of others, including Glaðheimr (Glad-home) and Valaskjálf (Shelf of the Slain) where Hliðskjálf (Opening-shelf), the high seat which lets him look out over the worlds, is situated.
- Transport: by eight-legged horse Sleipnir, but often travels on foot and in disguise.
- Animal associations: ravens (Huginn and Muninn, 'Thought' and 'Memory'); wolves (Geri and Freki, 'Ravener' and 'Devourer').
- Married to Frigg; numerous liaisons with giantesses and human women. Sons are Þórr, Baldr, Víðarr, Váli, Höðr.
- Particularly important in Denmark.

One-eyed Óðinn with his ravens and his spear Gungnir,
in an eighteenth-century Icelandic manuscript.

he's more of a strategist than a fighter, teaching his chosen heroes
effective battle-formations, including one shaped like a pig's snout,
the *svínfylking*. Óðinn stirs up conflict, so that he may see who is
worthy to enter his great hall Valhöll (Valhalla), to join the *Einherjar*,
the warriors who will fight with the gods at *ragnarök*. He decrees
defeat or victory in battle, and he is able to confer immunity to
wounds with his spear, although he sometimes sends his valkyries
to determine who will win or lose.

Óðinn is also the god of wisdom, and he seeks it out wherever it
may be found. He has sacrificed one of his eyes in Mímir's Well to
gain arcane knowledge, and he hanged himself on the World-Tree
Yggdrasill in order to win knowledge of the runes, the Germanic
writing system which enabled gods and men to record their knowledge for posterity.

Valkyries

Valkyries are supernatural women who dwell in Valhöll. They serve wine and mead to the warriors who live there. Another of their tasks is to ride out to battle, where they bestow victory or defeat, and their name means 'Choosers of the Slain'. Sometimes Óðinn instructs them as to who is to win, and sometimes they take the initiative in choosing who will accompany them back to Valhöll. Not all kings are thrilled to be invited to join the elite (but dead) warriors, rather than continuing to rule on earth. A memorial poem for the Norwegian King Hákon depicts him as distinctly sulky, even when the greatest heroes of the past welcome him to the hall. The valkyrie Brynhildr is punished by Óðinn for disobeying orders and giving victory to a younger and handsomer man. Some human girls also take up the valkyrie life as shield-maidens. This allows them to choose a heroic husband who can save them from marriage to an unwanted suitor, as we'll see in Chapter 4.

A valkyrie in full flight, sculpted by Stephan Sinding (1910).

Óðinn hanging himself on Yggdrasill. Illustration by W. G. Collingwood
for Olive Bray's 1908 translation of the *Poetic Edda*.

I know that I hung on a windswept tree
nine long nights,
wounded with a spear, dedicated to Óðinn,
myself to myself
on that tree of which no man knows
from where its roots run.

With no bread did they refresh me nor a drink from a horn,
downwards I peered;
I took up the runes, screaming I took them,
then I fell back from there.

SAYINGS OF THE HIGH ONE, VV. 138–39

Óðinn also knows spells to achieve various things: animating the dead, quenching fires, calling up winds. He lists eighteen of them in *Hávamál* (Sayings of the High One), but declines either to give details or to reveal the last one, which he won't tell any woman, unless it's his lover or his sister – and since there's no evidence for him having a sister, and he doesn't necessarily part on good terms with his lovers, that secret may be kept for a very long time indeed.

One of Óðinn's chief concerns is to find out as much as he can about *ragnarök*, the end of the world. To this end he visits various people in the divine and human worlds (see Chapters 5 and 6). He knows that the death of his son Baldr is one of the most significant portents of the end, but he hopes that – somehow – he can find a way of falsifying the prophecies about the catastrophe to come. He is also an accomplished practitioner of magic of a particularly disreputable kind called *seiðr* (see Chapter 2, page 84). We don't know much about what this entails, but it seems mainly to be the province of women. When men perform it, it involves cross-dressing: something that is inherently shameful in Norse culture. In fact, Óðinn and Loki have an exchange of words about it in the poem *Lokasenna* (Loki's Quarrel). When Óðinn accuses Loki of spending eight winters under the earth in the form of a milch-cow and a woman, bearing children there, Loki retorts that his blood-brother practised *seiðr* on the island of Sámsey (modern Samsø, lying between Sweden and Denmark) 'and beat on the drum as seeresses do'. Frigg quickly intervenes to tell the two gods not to discuss such mysterious, ancient matters in public.

Óðinn is also the patron of kings. We'll see in Chapter 4 how he takes an interest in human kings and heroes. He's keen to get his favourites onto the throne, and he also wants them to rule effectively. Yet, in line with his task of choosing the best heroes for Valhöll, he also oversees the death of kings and heroes, a role which they often regard as a betrayal. In some poems they reproach Óðinn when they arrive in Valhöll, claiming, correctly, that he is not to be trusted.

Runes

The runes are the Germanic writing system, which pre-dated the introduction of the Roman alphabet to the north with the coming of Christianity. The runes evolved at the very beginning of the first century CE, probably out of a version of the Roman alphabet, and perhaps in the Rhine area. The letters were adapted to be easy to carve on hard surfaces such as wood or stone. The older *futhark* (as the alphabet is called, after its first six letters) comprised twenty-four or twenty-five letters. Later the alphabet was simplified as the younger *futhark* in the late eighth century in Scandinavia. This contained only sixteen characters and the majority of surviving runic inscriptions use it. The runes represented a sound, such as 'b' or 'th', but each rune also had a name: 'f' was *fé* (money, property) for example. In Old Norse myth the runes have magical properties – Óðinn uses them to bewitch the princess Rindr (see Chapter 6). In the sagas there are cases of sick people getting worse because wrongly cut runes have been used to try to heal them.

The older *futhark*.

Þórr as thunder god, riding out in his goat-drawn chariot to smite giants with his hammer. Painting by Mårten Eskil Winge (1872).

Þórr's chief role is to defend the gods' realm against the depredations of giants. He spends much of his time journeying in the east, where he wages war with his mighty hammer Mjöllnir on giants and giantesses alike. He is the one god who forges a close relationship with humans; he has two servants, a boy and a girl, called Þjálfi and Röskva. Although Loki's giant affiliations should make Þórr highly suspicious of him, the two gods often adventure together. Þórr's opponent at *ragnarök* is the Miðgarðs-serpent, a child of Loki, who will rise out of the sea. Just as Óðinn is interested in discovering whether *ragnarök* is

Þórr

- Red-bearded, batterer of giants. Short-tempered and not especially clever. God of weather, of sea-faring (in Iceland), of the fields and crops; worshipped by farmers.
- Attributes: hammer Mjöllnir; a pair of iron gloves; the belt of divine power.
- Halls: Þrúðheimr (Vigour-home); Bilskírnir (with 540 doors).
- Transport: goat-drawn chariot.
- Animal associations: the goats Tanngnjóstr and Tanngrisnir (Tooth-gnasher; Tooth-grinder). These animals can be killed, eaten, and reconstituted the next morning.
- Married to Sif, the golden-haired; son of Jörð (Earth, a giantess), and Óðinn.
- Children: Magni and Móði and daughter Þrúðr. In one poem Þórr returns home to find his daughter betrothed to a hideous dwarf; the god tests the dwarf Alvíss (All-wise) in arcane lore until the sun comes up and he's turned to stone.
- Most important god in Norway and Iceland.

inevitable, Þórr too has an early face-off with the Miðgarðs-serpent (see Chapter 3 for the full story).

Not very much is known about Heimdallr. He is the divine watchman, keeping an eye open for the approach of enemies. He will blow his mighty horn at the onset of *ragnarök*. His hearing is – mysteriously – sunk in Mímir's Well, like Óðinn's eye, but this does not damage his capacity to keep watch, for his hearing is so keen that he can hear wool grow on a sheep's back. He's also responsible for establishing the social hierarchy among humans. The poem *Rígsþula* (Rígr's List) tells how, assuming the name Rígr (an Irish word for 'king'), Heimdallr goes walking through the human world. He comes to three houses in turn: one is a peasant hut, one a pleasant farmstead and one a noble hall. At each place, he is invited in, offered food and, for three nights, he sleeps between the married

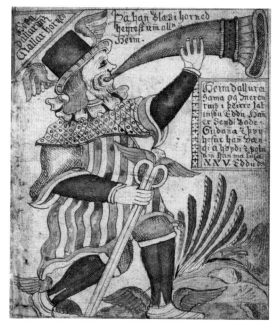

Heimdallr with the Gjallar-horn, which he will blow to signal the coming of *ragnarök*. From an eighteenth-century Icelandic manuscript.

Heimdallr
- Known as the white god; has golden teeth.
- Watchman of the gods who sits at the edge of the gods' domain. His back is always dirty from the mud cascading down Yggdrasill.
- Hearing is hidden in Mímir's Well at foot of Yggdrasill.
- Attribute: the great Gjallar-horn, blown at the onset of *ragnarök*.
- Hall: Himinbjörg (Heaven-refuge).
- Animal association: the horse Gulltoppr (Golden-forelock).
- Son of nine mothers, all sisters. Has fought in seal-form against Loki; they are fated to meet again in combat at *ragnarök* (see Chapter 6).

The radiant Baldr, believing himself invulnerable, allows the other gods to throw missiles at him. To the right, a hooded Loki puts the mistletoe dart into blind Höðr's hand (Chapter 6). Elmer Boyd Smith (1902).

Baldr
- Best and brightest of the gods; radiates light.
- Has remarkably blond eyelashes.
- Dies young. Will return after *ragnarök*.
- Hall: Breiðablikr (Broad-view).
- Married to Nanna, who goes to Hel with him.

couple in their bed. Each woman later gives birth to a child. The peasant couple's baby is Thrall, ugly, but brawny, and destined for manual labour. The farming couple's son is Karl, a well-to-do yeoman who works the land he owns, while the noble pair bring up Jarl, or Earl, a splendid young aristocrat. Jarl's youngest child is Konr *ungr*, 'young Konr', a phrase meaning 'king' (*konungr*). When Konr is of age, Rígr comes to teach him knowledge of runes. The poem breaks off as Konr is setting out to acquire a kingdom through battle.

Baldr has little to do in Norse myth, except to die; the story of his murder is related in Chapter 6. Of all the gods, he is the one who has the strongest kinship ties and when, before his death, he begins to have bad dreams, both his parents spring into action. He is accidentally slain by his brother, while his wife dies of grief at his funeral. It's foretold that he will come back to the dwellings of the gods after *ragnarök*. This piece of information is crucial for Óðinn, for it offers him hope that some of the gods will return to make the world anew.

Occupying a strange and ambivalent position, Loki has mixed parentage which makes his loyalties uncertain. He is Óðinn's blood-brother, and the highest god has sworn never to drink ale unless Loki is also offered a drink. Loki is always getting the gods into trouble, and thus often has to get them out again. His luck runs out when, through his boasting in the poem *Loki's Quarrel*, his role in the death of Baldr becomes clear, and he is captured and bound until *ragnarök*. On that day he will declare his final allegiance to the giants and march with them against the gods. Loki's mother seems to be a goddess and his father a giant, a match which runs contrary to normal divine marriage rules. His relationship with a giantess brings forth monstrous offspring. His gender is also subject to slippage: he's the mother of the eight-legged horse, Sleipnir (see Chapter 3); he becomes pregnant from eating a half-cooked female heart; and, as Óðinn claims, he seems to have spent eight winters underground as a woman.

Loki and his invention, the fishing-net, from an eighteenth-century Icelandic manuscript. A net such as this brings about Loki's capture (Chapter 6).

Loki
- Son of a goddess and a giant. Good-looking but nasty in temperament, and variable in behaviour. Exceptionally cunning, while his sexuality is distinctly polymorphous.
- Married to Sigyn. Has two sons. Snorri names them as Váli and Nari or Narfi; the *Poetic Edda* calls them Nari and Narfi. Father of these cosmic monsters by the giantess Angrboða: Fenrir the Mighty Wolf; the Miðgarðs-serpent; and Hel, goddess of death. Also the mother (see Chapter 3) of Sleipnir, Óðinn's eight-legged horse.

ᛟ THE VANIR ᛟ

The Vanir are an important subgroup of gods. How they came to be among the Æsir is explained in Chapter 2. There are four named Vanir: Njörðr and his two children Freyr and Freyja, who live in Ásgarðr, the realm of the gods, and Kvasir, the wisest of gods, who has a very chequered fate (see Chapter 3).

Njörðr releasing the winds, from a seventeenth-century Icelandic manuscript.

Njörðr

- One of the Vanir. God of the sea.
- Has oversight of fishermen and sea-journeys and hunting.
- Can quieten winds.
- Attributes: exceptionally clean feet. Not fond of the mountains.
- Hall: Nóatún (Ship-yard), by the seashore.
- Married to the giantess Skaði for a while. Father of Freyr and Freyja, allegedly by his sister.

Njörðr's chief claim to fame is his unsuccessful marriage to the giantess Skaði (see Chapter 3). The earlier incestuous relationship with his sister, on whom he fathered Freyr and Freyja, seems to be permitted among the Vanir; certainly his daughter is accused of having had sex with her brother, along with a good many other men. Njörðr shares the root of his name with Nerthus, a very ancient

Nerthus, an Early Germanic Deity

Nerthus, so Tacitus tells us, was the Mother Earth goddess of the Langobardi, a Germanic tribe who lived in northern Italy. Nerthus lived in a sacred grove on an island in a lake. On the island was a holy chariot which only the priest of Nerthus was allowed to touch. Around the chariot was a curtain, and on occasion the goddess would manifest herself behind it. At such times, the priest would lead the chariot, yoked to cows, among the people so that the goddess could visit them. No war or fighting was permitted while the goddess was on her travels; peace and happiness broke out. When the goddess's journey was over, chariot and cows, and perhaps the goddess herself, were washed by slaves in the sacred lake. Then the slaves were drowned in the same lake, 'a place of mysterious horror', Tacitus writes.

Nerthus is borne by her priests among the people. Emil Doepler (1905).

Freyr with his boar, Gullinbursti (Golden-bristle).
Johannes Gehrts (1901).

Freyr
- One of the Vanir. Handsome. Mentioned as a war-leader, but in Sweden he is chiefly in charge of crops, weather and harvests.
- Attributes: gave away his sword and must fight with a deer antler at *ragnarök*.
- Hall: Álfheimr (Elf-home).
- Transport: a fold-up boat, manufactured by dwarfs, called Skíðblaðnir.
- Animal association: the boar Gullinbursti (Golden-bristle).
- Married (or had a relationship with) Gerðr, a giantess. Son called Fjölnir. Possible sexual relationship with sister Freyja. Ancestor of the kings of Sweden.

Freyja, the beautiful golden-haired goddess of love.
John Bauer (1911).

Freyja
- One of the Vanir. Good to invoke in affairs of the heart, and very fond of love-songs. Chooses half the slain, along with Óðinn.
- Attributes: falcon-feather flying-cloak. Weeps tears of gold. Owns the *Brisinga men* neck-ring.
- Halls: Folkvangr (People-plain) and Søkkvabekkir (Sunken-benches).
- Transport: chariot drawn by cats.
- Married to Óðr, who has gone away on a journey, but has apparently slept with almost everyone, including her brother.

Germanic female deity mentioned by the Roman historian Tacitus, writing in 98 CE. Njörðr has clearly undergone a sex-change on his journey northwards, but the details of the Nerthus-cult match some of the archaeological evidence for the worship of wooden figures in the later Scandinavian Iron Age.

Freyr's name means simply 'Lord' and he has two roles. One, less often mentioned, is as a battle-leader, apparently a more hands-on fighter than Óðinn the tactician. He's called 'the gods' war-leader' and a 'bold rider' who redeems captives from their chains. His other role is as the god of fertility of beast and field. As ancestor of the kings of Sweden he brought good harvests and people sacrificed to him for prosperity. The story of his courtship of the giantess Gerðr (see Chapter 3) has often been thought to reflect the action of the sun-god on the earth in springtime. He also possesses a boar called Gullinbursti (Golden-bristle), capable of being ridden.

Freyja, whose name means 'Lady', is the goddess most closely associated with sexuality, though she also has some kind of authority over the dead. Her husband Óðr has gone off on a long journey and Freyja weeps tears of gold in his absence. Loki accuses her of having had sex with her brother – but then, as a fertility goddess associated with love-affairs, Freyja seems to have had sex with everyone: 'of the Æsir and the elves who are in here / each one has been your lover', claims Loki. And when the gods caught her in the act with Freyr, she was so alarmed that she farted! She is also a patron of humans and helps her protégé Óttarr to gain his inheritance, by questioning the giantess Hyndla (see Chapter 3).

Freyja's fondness for jewelry is evidenced by the price she was prepared to pay for the wonderful *Brisinga men* neck-ring (see pages 73–74). She is so pleased with her new treasure that she even wears it to bed. Freyja is said by Snorri to have two daughters, whose names are Gersemi and Hnoss. Both are words for 'treasure', cementing the goddess's association with gold.

☗ LESS IMPORTANT ÆSIR ☗

Týr, the one-handed god, gives victory in battle. He lost his hand in the jaws of the great wolf, Fenrir; how this came about is told in Chapter 3. He is associated with law and justice and, meanly, Loki twits him on his lack of even-handedness in this respect. Little more is known about him. His mother is apparently one of the Ásynjur, yet married to a rather unfriendly giant. Týr's name connects him

Týr, watched by Óðinn, places his hand in the mouth of Fenrir, as the fetter tightens around the wolf's paws. From an eighteenth-century Icelandic manuscript.

Víðarr, the 'silent god', attacks Fenrir (Chapter 6).
W. G. Collingwood (1908).

with both Zeus and Jupiter (they come from the same root), and perhaps he was originally a sky-god. In his Old English form, Tiw, he gives his name to Tuesday.

Höðr, the blind god, is the brother of Baldr. The gods prefer not to talk about him, it's said, because of his role in his brother's death. He will be killed by Váli in vengeance for Baldr's slaying. Höðr too will return in the glorious days after *ragnarök*, when 'all harms will be healed', and he will then live in peace with his brother.

Víðarr is known as the silent god and has thick-soled shoes. He will need these at *ragnarök* when he will have to avenge his father Óðinn by leaping into the maw of Fenrir the wolf and tearing his jaws apart.

Váli is born to avenge Baldr. How this comes about is narrated in Chapter 6.

Forseti is the go-to god for legal difficulties. He has the best judgment-place at his hall, known as Glitnir (Shining-place). He's Baldr's son, and his name is the title now given to the President of Iceland.

Ullr, on skis, with his bow, and perhaps the yew tree from which it was made. From an eighteenth-century Icelandic manuscript.

Ullr is the god of archery; he is an excellent skier and he's good to invoke if you're going to fight in single combat. He lives in Ýdalir (Yew-dales), fittingly, for yew-wood is excellent material for bow-making. He is the son of Sif, and thus the stepson of Þórr, but no one knows who his father is.

Finally, there is Bragi, who is the god of poetry, eloquence and language and is married to Iðunn. Bragi was, most likely, originally a human; one of the earliest named poets in Old Norse was called Bragi the Old, and some of his poems have been preserved. He seems to have been a late addition to the pantheon.

☒ THE ÁSYNJUR (GODDESSES) ☒

Frigg, Óðinn's wife, knows all about fate, even if she does not reveal her knowledge publicly. That her hall is called Fensalir (Fen-halls) suggests that she has an affinity with standing water, and it's possible that some of the early Iron Age sacrifices made by depositing precious objects in Danish bogs may have been intended to honour her. Frigg's Old English counterpart *Fricg* gives her name to Friday in English; Freyja is not known outside Scandinavia and so it is Fricg who has strong associations with sex in Anglo-Saxon England.

Sif is married to Þórr and had exceptionally beautiful golden hair. This was stolen by Loki – how is unclear, but he insinuates that he has slept with her, and that may have offered the opportunity for his theft. Sif wept for the loss of her locks, but Loki made amends with a dwarf-made substitute set of tresses. This wig grafted itself instantly onto Sif's head and was even lovelier than the original. 'Sif's hair' is thus a kenning for gold.

Iðunn, married to Bragi, is the guardian of the apples of eternal youth. The gods need to eat these regularly if they are to remain young and vigorous. When she and her apples are kidnapped by a scheming giant (see Chapter 3), the gods quickly fade and grow old. It's a situation which, as usual, Loki is responsible for creating and which he has to remedy through his habitual ingenuity.

Gefjun visited King Gylfi of Sweden in the guise of a wandering woman, and, as 'a reward for his entertainment', Gylfi agreed to let

---

Frigg
- Most important of the goddesses.
- Patron of love and marriage.
- Attributes: knows all fate. Also said to have a feather flying-cloak.
- Hall: Fensalir (Fen-halls).
- Married to Óðinn, mother of Baldr. Her serving-maid is Fulla.

Gefjun drives the plough with her four giant sons transformed into oxen in order to create the Danish island of Sjælland. Statue sculpted in 1897–99 by Anders Bundgaard for a fountain in Copenhagen.

her have some land – as much as four oxen could plough in a day and a night. This might have constituted a decent-sized farm, but in fact Gefjun had four giant sons. They were transformed into oxen and managed, in their twenty-four-hour ploughing marathon, to carve out a huge hole in Gylfi's territory. The hole is now Sweden's third largest lake, Lake Mälaren, and the land that they dragged away has formed the Danish island of Sjælland, where Copenhagen now stands. Gefjun, Snorri tells us, is a virgin and the patron of virgins, which doesn't exactly square with the giant-son tale. Like Frigg, Gefjun is said to know all about fate.

Skaði, a giantess and warrior woman, is the goddess of hunting and skiing. Her hall is Þrymheimr (Þrymr's home – Þrymr is a giant), inherited from her father Þjazi.

When Skaði marches, fully armoured and brandishing her weapons, into Ásgarðr, she's seeking compensation for the death of Þjazi at the hands of the gods (see Chapter 3). On that occasion she's sweet-talked into accepting a husband from among the gods, with the proviso that she must choose from a range of candidates hidden

Skaði in her mountain habitat, hunting on skis.
Drawn by 'H.L.M.' (1901).

behind a sheet. Since only their feet are visible, she ends up selecting Njörðr, the god associated with the sea – whose feet are, of course, remarkably bright and clean! Skaði is displeased for she had hoped to win Baldr as husband, but she's persuaded by Loki that if he can make her laugh, she will accept the situation. Grim-faced Skaði is in no mood for amusement, but Loki ties a goat by the beard to his testicles and each of them pulls in different directions. 'Both of them screeched very loudly at that,' Snorri says. Loki tumbles into Skaði's lap and, finally, she laughs. The sexualized burlesque has done its work, though, as we'll see, the marriage between Skaði and Njörðr is not a successful one.

Fulla, Frigg's handmaiden, wears her hair loose and has charge of the goddess's shoe collection. Fulla is a very old goddess; she appears in a charm in Old High German, recorded in the tenth century.

A Charm Used by the Gods

In the so-called 'Second Merseburg Charm', Baldr, Woden, Friia (Frigg) and Volla (Fulla) are mentioned along with some other unidentified figures: Phol, Sinthgut and Sunna. Phol and Woden were riding to the woods when Baldr's horse sprained its foot. The female deities and Woden conjured the foot to knit together: 'bone to bone, blood to blood, joint to joint'. The limb was healed and, the spell suggests, the same incantation can be used for curing other creatures. This little story is a mythic memory, invoking the gods' effective actions to bring about healing in the present.

Frigg and her handmaidens, with Baldr and Óðinn, tend to Baldr's injured horse. Emil Doepler (1905).

Now that the gods and goddesses have been introduced, it's time to look at the myths in which they appear. We begin at the very beginning of Time, with the origins of the gods and the creation of the world, in the next chapter.

2

~~~~~~~

CREATING AND CRAFTING
THE WORLD

Early in time Ymir made his settlement,
there was no sand nor sea nor cool waves;
earth was nowhere nor the sky above,
a void of yawning chaos, grass was there nowhere

Before the sons of Burr brought up the land surface,
those who shaped glorious Midgard.
THE SEERESS'S PROPHECY, VV. 3–4

Creating a universe where nothing exists but *ginnunga gap*, a gaping void, isn't an easy task. Creator-gods need resourcefulness and planning to bring a world into existence, and they also need material from which to construct their creation. The Jewish–Christian God speaks creation into existence through the Word, the *Logos*. When he commands 'Let there be light', light springs into being and his words power the rest of the creation process. In other creation mythologies female figures give birth to the world; sky and earth lie together and all that is, is born of that union. Old Norse has at least three active creation myths; each tells us something different about the ways in which creation might be imagined as coming to pass. The version cited above suggests that the sons of Burr (Óðinn and his brothers Vili and Vé) summoned the land up from the *ginnunga gap*. In the lines which follow in *Völuspá* (The Seeress's Prophecy), green leeks (a superior kind of grass) begin to grow on the rocky ground, and the task of world-shaping seems already to be complete.

Offering his own elaboration, based on medieval scientific theory, Snorri explains creation as a synthesis of oppositions. Ginnunga gap, he tells us, is a place that lies in the north: an ice-filled chasm sprung from a river called Élivágar whose poisonous flow had solidified into frost and ice. The land of fire, Muspellsheimr, domain of the fire-giant Surtr, lies to the south. And when the sparks that flew up from Muspellsheimr landed upon the ice of Ginnunga gap, it began to melt, and life – generated from the union of the heat and dryness of fire and the cold and moistness of ice – was engendered in the shape of a man. He's named both as Aurgelmir and as Ymir, the progenitor of the frost-giants. As Ymir slept, he sweated, and from under his armpits sprang up a male and a female. His two feet also produced a child with one another: these were the first giants.

Whether the sons of Burr called the earth up from the depths, or dived down and fetched it up, is not clear from the account above. But Old Norse tradition offers a second creation method: one involving violence and dismemberment. The sons of Burr laid hands on the *Ur*-giant Ymir, killed him and used his body parts to form the different parts of the world, according to *Grímnir's Sayings*:

The sons of Burr create the world by lifting it up from the primeval chasm.
Lorenz Frølich (1895).

Auðhumla, the primeval cow, licks Burr out of the ice.
From an eighteenth-century Icelandic manuscript.

A Cosmic Cow

A cosmic cow called Auðhumla appeared from the ice and she
nourished Ymir with her milk. As she licked the salty rime-stone, the
figure of a handsome and powerful man called Búri began to appear.
Búri was the father of Borr (another name for Burr), and *he* fathered
Óðinn and his brothers Vili and Vé. What happened to Auðhumla
afterwards, we don't know. Perhaps she wandered off to graze the new
grass springing on the emerging earth. Auðhumla may have had some
descendants, for later stories tell us about sacred cows who were
important to pre-Christian kings.

From Ymir's flesh the earth was made,
and from his blood, the sea,
mountains from his bones, trees from his hair,
and from his skull, the sky.

And from his eyelashes the cheerful gods
made Miðgarðr for men's sons;
and from his brain the hard-tempered clouds
were all created.
GRÍMNIR'S SAYINGS, VV. 40–41

The world in which humans live (Miðgarðr, the 'middle-place'), then, is constructed from the body of a murdered being, created through violence and savagery, in a creative act which is an all-male affair. The Old Norse myths are very much related from the point of view of the Æsir – that is, the male gods – and in the matter of creation they appropriate the powers of giving life, nurturing and fertility that are normally gendered female. Unlike women, the gods cannot make the material they need for creation from their own bodies and so they must take matter where they can find it. In weaving aggression into the very fabric of the universe, the gods incorporate and endorse violence among humans and gods. Whether this version of the creation myth is the more ancient, or whether it is a cultural product of the warring centuries of the early Iron Age or even the Viking Age, we cannot know. It may be significant that the more peaceable (if still exclusively male) creative act of bringing the land up out of the sea is recounted in *The Seeress's Prophecy*, a poem now thought to have been composed around the year 1000, when Christian ideas were already strongly percolating through Nordic mythological thinking.

⚹ SETTING UP TIME ⚹

Once the world has been constituted and space has been defined and mapped out, the gods' next move is to regulate the heavenly bodies. Sun, moon and stars already seem to exist, but they have no set course through the skies. The deities meet in solemn conclave and establish the subdivisions of time:

> *to night and her children they gave names,*
> *morning they named and midday*
> *afternoon and evening, to reckon up in years.*
> THE SEERESS'S PROPHECY, V. 6, LL. 5–10

The sun and moon are imagined in different ways. One tradition says that they speed through the sky because devouring wolves are on their tracks; these wolves, probably avatars of the cosmic wolf Fenrir, will catch and consume them at *ragnarök*. Elsewhere the heavenly bodies are borne in chariots, driven by figures whose

Bronze-Age model of a sun-chariot, dated between 1800 and 1600 BCE, from Trundholm, Denmark.

names are related to Day and Night and drawn by horses called Skínfaxi (Shining-mane) and Hrímfaxi (Frost-mane). Now that time has been established, the gods are liable for its unforeseen consequences. The emergence of past, present and future brings uncertainty and some loss of power. For the giants have longer and better memories of the past than those gods who represent the third and fourth generations of descendants from the *Ur*-giant, and they guard that knowledge jealously. Nor is the future perspicuous to the gods; prophetesses and certain giants have clearer knowledge of what is to come than most of the Æsir. Although the goddesses Gefjun and Frigg are said to know fate, they do not reveal what they know. The quest to discover the future, to find out the details of *ragnarök* and perhaps to discern whether it can be averted, is one of Óðinn's abiding obsessions, as we'll see in Chapter 6.

By evolving a time-system which operates within cycles (the recurrent cycles of days and years and the larger cycle of creation, *ragnarök* and rebirth), the gods have invited the emergence of fate: future events in the existence of individuals and social groups that may be foreseen, but cannot be prevented. The gods themselves are subject to fate and must obey its laws.

The Three Fate-Maidens

Under Yggdrasill, the World-Tree, is a hall or a spring (or, conceivably, a hall by a spring). Here dwell the three fate-maidens, Urðr, Verðandi and Skuld; they are said to cut wooden slips on which individual destinies are incised. Urðr has an ancient name, related to *wyrd*, the Old English word for 'destiny' and the antecedent of modern English *weird*. Verðandi represents the present, for the form of her name is a present participle (Becoming) while Skuld (Must-be) seems to evoke the future. A stoical acceptance of how fate operates is crucial for the hero to fulfil his destiny, as we'll see in Chapters 4 and 5.

A rendering of the Norse mythic universe, with Yggdrasill growing up through Ásgarðr, and the worlds of men, giants and the dead clustered at its roots, in Bishop Percy's *Northern Antiquities* (1847).

ᛉ THE MYTHIC LANDSCAPE ᛉ

Once space has been shaped and time established we are in a position to describe the geography of the Norse mythic universe. Central is Yggdrasill, the World-Tree, the great ash whose roots, usually three in number, define the different regions of the world.

> *Three roots there grow in three directions*
> *under Yggdrasill's ash;*
> *Hel lives under one, under the second, the frost-giants,*
> *under the third, humankind.*
> GRÍMNIR'S SAYINGS, V. 31

Heiðrún the goat stands on the roof of Valhöll, cropping the leaves of Yggdrasill. A vessel to hold the mead that flows from her udders is nearby. From an eighteenth-century Icelandic manuscript.

Snorri agrees that the world of the dead, Niflheimr (Mist-world), ruled over by Loki's daughter Hel, lies under one root and that the second descends into the former Ginnunga gap, the icy realm of the frost-giants, but he replaces the human world with the world of gods, Ásgarðr in his model. Miðgarðr is the world of men, a central space, echoed in the Old English term *Middangeard*, 'earth', imagined as lying between heaven and hell in the Christian world-view (compare J. R. R. Tolkien's Middle Earth). Yet although the different worlds are said to lie below the place where the tree emerges from the ground, the neighbouring realms of gods and giants are also imagined as occupying a horizontal plane, with Jötunheimar (the Giantlands) lying in the mountainous east. Ásgarðr is envisaged as the centre of the cosmos; Óðinn's huge hall, Valhöll, is situated within it, under Yggdrasill. A goat

The animals of Yggdrasill: the eagle and hawk perched at the top, the four stags along the sides, Ratatöskr the squirrel at bottom left and the dragon Níðhöggr gnawing the roots from beneath. From an eighteenth-century Icelandic manuscript.

called Heiðrún stands on its roof and grazes on the ash-tree. From her udders comes the unending supply of mead which sustains Valhöll's inhabitants, the *Einherjar*, the heroic human dead.

Heiðrún is not the only animal to be associated with Yggdrasill. The tree's name means 'Steed of the Terrible One', an epithet which derives from the story of Óðinn's sacrifice (see Chapter 1); in Germanic thinking, there's a well-established metaphor that understands the gallows as the horse ridden by the criminal who is hanged from it. Up in the tree's leafy crown, four stags browse on the young growth. Down below, serpents gnaw at the roots. An eagle roosts at the top of the tree, with a hawk perching between his eyes, and a squirrel with the wonderfully onomatopœic name of Ratatöskr runs up and down the trunk, bringing news from the worlds above and below. Among the serpents is the most dread creature of all, the dragon Níðhöggr (Hostile-hewer) who sometimes takes flight through the mythic world; he is a portent of horror. These creatures all take their toll on the tree, symbolizing the action of time as eroding its essence, eating into the symbolic axis of the world round which everything revolves. Though the stags are aristocratic in their associations and the goat is nurturing, they wear away at the tree just like the more obviously evil snakes.

Yggdrasill also shelters under its canopy Mímir's Well (see page 83, later in this chapter), and perhaps also the body of water by which the fates dwell. Shining white mud cascades down the tree, apparently onto Heimdallr, for Loki accuses him of having 'a mucky back'. Also located in the Well, it's said, are Heimdallr's hearing and Óðinn's eye, pledged in exchange for a drink from its waters. The two key organs sacrificed by the gods (the third, Týr's hand, doubtless gulped down by Fenrir when he bit it off, is irrecoverable) remain close at hand, still

---

Supernatural Females: Norns and *Dísir*

Several supernatural female figures are associated with fate. The norns have different functions; some are hostile, others help out with childbirth, others determine fate for a newborn child. Heroes often talk about 'the judgment of the norns' when at the point of death, realizing that their fatal hour has come. The *dísir* are a collective group of spirits, thought to be female ancestors, who bring death to kings and heroes. In one Icelandic tale a young man is warned not to step out into the farmyard one night, but he does so. In the sky he sees a group of nine dark-clad women and a group of nine white-clad women, symbolizing the old beliefs and the new Christian religion. Before the youth can go back into the farmhouse to report what he has seen, the dark-clad women attack him, and he dies after recounting his experience. A prophetic Norwegian identifies the dark women as *dísir* associated with the family and farm, who will abandon the lineage when Christianity comes.

The three norns, fateful supernatural females, by the well beneath Yggdrasill.
Lorenz Frølich (1895).

perhaps wired into their former owners. For the logic of sacrificial exchange – that something given up is rewarded by a better, enhanced return – suggests that Heimdallr's keen hearing and Óðinn's insight, if not his literal sight, stem from the power of the Well's living water.

Beyond Valhöll and its immediate surrounds, each deity has his or her own great hall, a place of authority and rulership, much like the chieftain-halls of the Viking Age excavated at Gamla Uppsala in Sweden, Lejre in Denmark or even the now-reconstructed hall of Eiríkr the Red at Brattahlíð in Greenland. Óðinn lists twelve such halls in the poem *Grímnismál* (Grímnir's Sayings), each owned by a particular god. The names of these dwellings bespeak light, splendour, joyfulness, or particular attributes of the god, such as Yewdales where the archer-god Ullr lives; yew-wood was a prime choice for bow-making. Óðinn's account evokes the gods' activities when enthroned in their halls: drinking, making judgments and assuaging quarrels, riding horses, and – perhaps ominously – choosing the slain, the divine equivalent of recruiting new followers to the chieftain's retinue.

Reconstructed hall of Eiríkr the Red at Brattahlíð, Greenland. The Norse gods were thought to inhabit similar halls of their own.

Out beyond where the giants live is the ocean. At its most distant edge, marking the boundary of the known world, lies the Miðgarðs-serpent, Jörmungandr, the Mighty Staff, awaiting its combat with Þórr. Below the ocean's depths lives Ægir, lord of the sea, perhaps a giant, perhaps a god, with his wife Rán, whose name means 'robbery' (the first element of our word 'ransack'). Rán seeks men's lives, catching them in her net and dragging them down to the depths. Her daughters with Ægir are the waves, sometimes tossing their heads with calm and peaceful demeanours, sometimes towering dangerously over the boats they intend to smash to matchwood.

That it is Ægir's wife and daughters who threaten sailors, that death at sea is gendered female, aligns with a culture-wide perception that the valkyries, the *dísir*, the norns and Hel herself, ruler of the world of the dead, all embody Death as a desiring woman, one who intends to take the moribund man as her lover in the next world and who longs to hold him in her fatal embrace. Just as women give birth, so they stand at the end of life, waiting for the doomed man to come into their arms. The great tenth-century Icelandic poet Egill Skalla-Grímsson ends his tragic poem *Sonatorrek* (On the Loss of Sons) with this verse:

Rán, goddess of the sea, carved as the figurehead to the *Jylland*,
a restored nineteenth-century Danish frigate.

Now it's difficult for me;
the sister of Óðinn's enemy [= Fenrir; Fenrir's sister = Hel]
stands on the headland;
yet glad, with good will,
and unafraid I shall wait
for Hel.
ON THE LOSS OF SONS, V. 25

☒ MAKING CULTURE ☒

We left the gods at the point when the world was all new and Day
and Night had just embarked on their regulated routes through the
heavens. There is still work to do to make the fresh, green world fit
for gods to live in, and so they set to:

The gods met on Idavoll Plain,
high they built altars and temples;
they set up their forges, smithed precious things,
shaped tongs and made tools.
THE SEERESS'S PROPHECY, V. 7

Once the places where they will be worshipped are completed, they turn to manufacture, making use of the ample valuable metals available to them. Civilization is inaugurated, perhaps as in Viking-Age towns such as Birka in Sweden and Hedeby (now north Germany), with the building of cult centres and of workshops. The Æsir also make luxury goods for themselves. When their work is done, they relax:

> *They played chequers in the meadow, they were merry,*
> *they did not lack for gold at all,*
> *until three ogre-girls came,*
> *all-powerful women, out of Giantlands.*
> THE SEERESS'S PROPHECY, V. 8

Remember those chequers – they will turn out to be important later. The 'until' is both crucial and mysterious here, for in the wake of the ogre-girls' arrival, the gods meet in what seems to be emergency session and decide to create the dwarfs, presumably to counteract the sudden shortage of gold. For dwarfs are underground creatures; it's beneath the earth's surface that they make the golden treasures which the gods covet – and are willing to pay for. How did the girls cause the loss of gold? Was it wagered away to them in a chequers game? Did

---

Tolkien's Dwarf Names

J. R. R. Tolkien took the names of most of his dwarfs in *The Hobbit* from the list in *The Seeress's Prophecy*. Dvalinn, Óin and Glóin, Fíli and Kíli, Dori, Nori and Ori, Bifur, Bofur and Bombur all have counterparts among Bilbo the hobbit's tea-party guests. Thorin Oakenshield, their leader, has two dwarf-names to his credit. Durinn and Thrain, also traditional Norse dwarf-names, are among the dwarfs' ancestors. Gandálfr also appears as a dwarf-name in the poem, a name which means 'Staff-elf' and which works, as Tolkien perceived, much better as a wizard-name: Gandalf the Grey.

The dwarfs forging Mjöllnir. Óðinn's spear Gungnir, Gullin-bursti the boar,
Skíðblaðnir the ship and the ring Draupnir are all visible in the foreground
while Þórr looks on approvingly. Elmer Boyd Smith (1902).

someone overturn the board in a fit of fury and thus lose the pieces?
When the giantess Skaði came marching into Ásgarðr she was seeking
recompense for the killing of her father Þjazi. The ogre-girls might
likewise be claiming a settlement for the death of their ancestor Ymir,
but one thing is certain: with their arrival, the golden age is over.

The dwarfs are swiftly created – Snorri tells us that they quick-
ened in the earth like maggots in flesh, a horribly vivid image – and
he draws on the catalogue of dwarf-names found in *The Seeress's
Prophecy* to list them all.

The dwarfs live either underground or in the rocks and they
work away at forging metal and crafting precious things. Some of
the gods' most important treasures are dwarf-made, such as Freyr's
folding ship Skíðblaðnir, the golden tresses of Sif, which replace
the hair stolen by Loki, and Óðinn's spear Gungnir. These were all

Carving of Loki's face from Snaptun, Denmark (*c.* 1000). The marks of the
stitches across the god's mouth are plainly visible.

manufactured by dwarf-brothers, the sons of Ívaldi. Another dwarf,
Brokkr, wagered with Loki that he and his brother could make three
equally good treasures; the stake was Loki's head. This competition was a close-run thing, for Brokkr and his brother created the
golden-bristled boar Gullinbursti, on which Freyr rides (thus taking
care of Vanir interests), the golden ring Draupnir, which drops from
itself eight equally heavy rings every ninth night (given to Óðinn)
and Þórr's great hammer, Mjöllnir. Loki tried hard to sabotage the
process, by transforming himself into a buzzing horse-fly and sting-
ing the craftsmen. They managed to ignore the persistent pest except
during the final task: forging Mjöllnir. The momentary distraction
was enough to cause the hammer's handle to come out a bit short.
Nonetheless, the jury of the gods agreed that Mjöllnir was so superior a giant-smashing treasure that Brokkr was the clear winner, and
that Loki must yield up his head. The ingenious god wriggled out of

Freyja finds the dwarfs forging the *Brisinga men* neck-ring.
Louis Huard (1891).

his fate by stipulating that Brokkr might take his head, but not his neck, and since not even a dwarf was dexterous enough to accomplish this, Loki was spared. But Brokkr brought it about that Loki's mouth was sewn up instead, so that he might not perform further verbal trickery, and thereafter the god has had a crooked mouth. And that's an image that isn't altogether inappropriate for someone known as *rœgjandi goðanna* (the bad-mouther of the gods).

A very late tale, dating from the fourteenth century, one which also alleges that Freyja is Óðinn's mistress, relates how that highly desirable treasure, the *Brisinga men* (neck-ring of the Brisings) came into the goddess's possession. Freyja is walking one day past a rock where some dwarfs live, and, noticing the rock-door open, she goes inside. There she sees that four dwarfs, including Dvalinn (known from other sources), are crafting a wonderful golden neck-ring. 'Freyja really liked the look of the neck-ring,' says the tale-narrator, 'and the dwarfs really liked the look of Freyja'. The goddess offers gold and silver in abundance in exchange for the *Brisinga men*, but the dwarfs are adamant about the price. Freyja must spend a night with each of them, and to this she reluctantly agrees. After four nights the neck-ring is hers.

Óðinn demands that Loki steal the treasure for him, and he buzzes in fly-form into Freyja's otherwise impenetrable chamber. She is sleeping with her new acquisition around her neck, lying on top of the clasp, and so Loki, transforming himself now into a flea, has to bite her very precisely in order to get her to turn over without waking up. Freyja stirs in her sleep, and the *Brisinga men* is soon in Loki's hands – and subsequently Óðinn's. When Freyja comes to Óðinn to complain of the theft and that her securely locked chamber (surely a sexual metaphor) has been violated, Óðinn agrees to return it to her on one condition: Freyja must set up the eternal conflict between two armies traditionally known as the Hjaðningavíg (the battle of the Hjaðnings), discussed in Chapter 5. Freyja agrees and the neck-ring is returned to her. This late tale incorporates two much older traditions – Loki's theft of the *Brisinga men* and the Hjaðningavíg battle – in a new Christianized framework. The conflict is meant to last until *ragnarök*, thanks to the revivification of the dead every night by Hildr, a woman whose name means 'Battle'; but in this version Óðinn foretells that it will last only until the great Christian king, Óláfr Tryggvason of Norway, comes to Orkney and puts an end to the strife.

⚔ THE GREATEST SMITH OF ALL ⚔

Skilful as the dwarfs are at making magical treasures for the gods to use, there's another smith, not a dwarf, who is so famous for his craftsmanship that his name is known in Scandinavia, Britain and Germany. Völundr, Wayland the Smith in English, Wieland in

German, is said, in the eddic poem which recounts his story, to have been a 'prince of elves'. Völundr marries a swan-maiden, one of three sisters, and he forges a good number of rings. But after nine winters spent together, the swan-maiden bride flies away. Völundr goes out to search for her, and in his absence King Níðuðr's men raid his home and steal one of the rings. On his return, Völundr counts his rings and believes his wife must have returned; lowering his guard he falls asleep and is easily captured by Níðuðr's troops. Völundr is taken to the king, and the mistrustful queen, who doesn't like the savage gleam in the captive's eyes, orders: 'Cut from him the might of his sinews / And afterwards put him in Sævarstaðr!' (*Völundr's Poem*, v. 17). So too, the highly allusive Old English version of the smith's history, preserved in the poem *Deor*, tells us that:

> *Weland, among serpents, got to know misery,*
> *the single-minded warrior experienced hardship,*
> *he had as companions sorrow and longing,*
> *winter-cold misery, often found woes*
> *after Niðhad laid on him in compulsion*
> *supple sinew-bonds on the better man.*
> DEOR, V. 1

Völundr is hamstrung, the tendons of his legs severed, and he is confined to an island where he is to slave for his captor, crafting treasures – jewelry, goblets, weapons. But Völundr turns the tables on Níðuðr. The king's inquisitive sons make the short boat-trip over to the island to see the smith at work and to admire the treasure. Völundr tells them to come again, secretly; when they do, he murders them and transforms their body parts into adornments. The word used in Old Norse for 'skulls', *skálar*, puns on the word for 'drinking-bowls', and also the word for 'Cheers!' (*skál*) in modern Icelandic:

He cut off the heads of those young cubs,
and under the mud of the forge he laid their limbs;
and their skulls, which were under their hair,
he chased in silver, gave to Níðuðr.

And the precious stones from their eyes,
he sent to Níðuðr's cunning wife;
and from the teeth of the two
he struck round brooches; sent them to Böðvildr.

VÖLUNDR'S POEM, VV. 24–25

Böðvildr, the boys' sister, also comes to visit Völundr, bringing his wife's ring which she has broken. Völundr offers to mend it, but he also plies her with beer, rapes or seduces her (the text is unclear), and she leaves the island, weeping piteously. Somehow, possession of the ring enables Völundr to escape and he flies away, pausing only to confront Níðuðr and to reveal the terrible truth. In Old English, Beadohild (Böðvildr) is rather more traumatized by her pregnancy than by the death of her brothers:

The Franks Casket

The eighth-century whalebone ivory casket known as the Franks Casket depicts scenes from this legend on its front. Framed with riddling runes referring to the material from which the box is made, a bearded Völundr with bent legs (from the hamstringing) offers the fateful beer to Böðvildr while her handmaid watches impassively. A dead body can be seen under the forge on which Völundr is shaping a treasure with his tongs. The activity of the man to the right of the scene, apparently strangling birds, is unclear as far as the English and eddic traditions are concerned. In a later Norse prose version, *Þiðreks Saga* (The Saga of Þiðrekr), the hero's brother comes to his rescue and helps him to build a pair of wings like those made by the Greek craftsman Daedalus; this might explain Völundr's suddenly acquired capacity to fly.

For Beadohild her brothers' death
was not so grievous to her spirit as her own plight,
when she had clearly perceived
that she was pregnant; she could never think
resolutely about what should come of that.

DEOR, V. 2

The eddic poem ends with the sobbing Böðvildr explaining herself to her father; the later saga account tells how Völundr (here called Vélent) returns with an army, crushes Níðuðr and marries Böðvildr: their son turns out to be a well-known Germanic hero. As for the Old English tale, this concludes with the enigmatic refrain, *þæs ofereode, þisses swa mæg* (That passed by, so may this). The poet who calls himself 'Deor' (Dear One or Animal) draws comfort for his own unhappy plight by considering how past miseries have turned to later happiness.

Weland (as he's known in Old English) becomes a byword for skilled craftsmanship; in *Beowulf* the hero's mailshirt is praised as *Welandes geweorc* (Weland's work). In South Oxfordshire up on the

Völundr the smith, depicted on the eighth-century Anglo-Saxon Franks Casket. The bearded smith passes a cup of beer to Böðvildr. Beneath the forge is the corpse of one of her brothers.

The so-called Wayland's Smithy, a Neolithic long barrow and chamber tomb, just off the Ridgeway in Oxfordshire.

Ridgeway is a Neolithic chamber-grave known as Wayland's Smithy, and local tradition had it that if you left your horse there with a silver penny, Weland would shoe it for you.

☿ WHY PEOPLE ARE TREES ☿

The gods preside over a world which they share with dwarfs, giants, elves (about whom very little is known) and a few monsters, the off-spring of Loki and a giantess named Angrboða. So far, there are no humans, no one to sacrifice to or to venerate the deities. One day, three gods, Óðinn, Hœnir and Lóðurr, were out walking, perhaps on the seashore, when they found some wood, 'capable of little / Askr and Embla, lacking in fate'. The three gods take it upon themselves to shape the ash-trunk and the other piece of timber (the meaning of Embla is not clear, though it has sometimes been connected with 'elm'). The lifeless logs are endowed with what they need to become human:

> *breath gave Óðinn, spirit gave Hœnir,*
> *blood gave Lóðurr, and fresh complexions.*
> THE SEERESS'S PROPHECY, V. 18

Lóðurr's identity is unknown; this verse is the only place that he is mentioned. Snorri expands on the gifts which the three gods lavish on the proto-humans, but simply names the creators as sons of Burr:

the first gave them breath and life, the second, wits and movement, the third, faces, speech, hearing and vision; they gave them names and clothes.
THE TRICKING OF GYLFI, CH. 23

Lóðurr has sometimes been identified with Loki, largely on the grounds of alliteration. Hœnir was traded to the Vanir (see below) as a hostage, but very little else is known about him. It's surprising, perhaps, that such obscure figures should have a hand in shaping the first humans, but these gods belong to the first divine genera-tion, it appears, and thus, like those Greek gods who preceded the Olympians, their characters and attributes may have faded over time. It is also the case that the surviving Norse myths are not par-ticularly interested in human beings. The gods rarely encounter them, although Þórr acquires a couple of human servants. Only Óðinn, with his project of populating Valhöll with the *Einherjar*, the finest human heroes, to fight alongside the gods at *ragnarök*, interacts much with them. He appears in order to advise, warn and finally betray them in their last battles. As patron of wisdom Óðinn also journeys among mankind, acquiring different kinds of knowledge, collected up in the poem *Sayings of the High One*. In this poem Óðinn travels alone through the human world, learning such truths as the blessings of friendship and the importance of mod-eration in eating and drinking. His propensity to travel in disguise accounts for his role in later Christian stories as a tempter, visiting pious Norwegian kings in order to deceive them into behaving in an unchristian fashion.

Humans do not forget that they were originally shaped from trees. This metaphorical understanding determines a number of

---

Óðinn the Tempter

King Óláfr Tryggvason is staying at a hall in northern Norway just before
Easter. A mysterious stranger appears at the hall and keeps the king up
late into the night, telling stories about the kings and heroes of the past.
The bishop suggests that it's time for sleep, but the king wants to hear
more. When he awakens, almost oversleeping and missing Mass, the
stranger has vanished. But the king learns that, before he went, the
stranger had been in the kitchens, made rude remarks about the quality
of the meat intended for the Easter feast, and left a side of meat to be
served up instead. Since the stranger had told a tale of King Dixin, a ruler
of the ancient past who had had a sacred cow and had been buried with
it, the suggestion is that the meat comes from the 200-years-dead beast.
Disgusting! The king realizes that the tempter and teller of old tales was
none other than Óðinn, seeking to lead him astray, by inviting him to
admire figures of the pagan past and by trying to make him miss Mass.

---

skaldic kennings: men are habitually designated with variants of
'tree of weapons' or 'tree of battle'. The valkyrie Sigrdrífa addresses
the hero Sigurðr as 'apple-tree of battle' – quite apposite given that
a magic apple was key to the conception of one of Sigurðr's ancestors (see Chapter 4). Helgi, slayer of Hundingr, is, as a young prince,
called 'the splendidly-born elm'. Women too are 'trees' or 'props of
gold' or 'poles of drink', referring to their role in providing hospitality. In skaldic poetry there are woman-kennings such as 'the
foremost birch of the fire of the sea' (fire of the sea = gold) or 'the
wine-oak'. The shield-maiden Brynhildr is called a 'neck-ring-tree'.
In heroic poetry, Guðrún, Sigurðr's wife, makes creative use of the
trope to describe her misery at her husband's murder: 'I am as little
as a leaf / among the bay-willows now my prince is dead'; later in
her career she laments her loss of kinfolk:

> I have come to stand alone like an aspen in the forest,
> my kinsmen cut away like a fir's branches,

bereft of happiness, as a tree of its leaves,
when the branch-breaker comes on a warm day.
LAY OF HAMÐIR, V. 5

Although trees cannot move, their strength and uprightness, their participation in annual cycles, and their longevity and eventual death, by disease, fire, or the woodsman's axe, makes them powerful comparators for human existence. Trees represent what humans aspire to be: beautiful, dignified, strong and enduring. The fact that humans are also, in little, slips from the World-Tree, ash saplings of Yggdrasill, underlines the interconnectedness of mythic tree-concepts. The great tree, subject like the rest of us to time and mortality, nevertheless spreads its protecting branches over gods and men, while the smaller trees, like Guðrún above, lose their branches and finally fall.

⚔ THE ARRIVAL OF THE VANIR ⚔

The gods are barely, it seems, settled in Ásgarðr when a new set of divinities appears on the scene: the Vanir. The Vanir may have been the original, local gods of Scandinavia and the Æsir the interlopers, arriving along with the Indo-Europeans during the Bronze Age, but we lack evidence to determine who had priority in the Norse cultic world. In our texts though, it's very clear that the Æsir are the dominant group; the history of the gods is an Æsir-centric one.

The impact of the Vanir is heralded by the appearance of Gullveig, a female figure who somehow falls foul of the Æsir. She is stuck with spears and consumed by fire:

... in the High-One's hall they burned her
three times they burned her, three times she was reborn,
over and over, and yet she lives still.
THE SEERESS'S PROPHECY, V. 21

Gullveig is stabbed with spears and three times set ablaze by the Æsir.
Lorenz Frølich (1895).

Gullveig (Gold-Liquor) is also known as 'Bright One' (Heiðr) and in this form she is said to visit houses and teach the magical practices of *seiðr*; she was always popular with wicked women for this reason, so *The Seeress's Prophecy* tells us. Who is this unkillable woman? There's no further information in other sources; our best guess is that she represents a version of Freyja. She is not one of the Æsir, she has the power of revivification, and she knows a forbidden form of magic: all this points to the chief goddess of the Vanir. So Snorri seems to conclude, for he characterizes Freyja in *The Saga of the Ynglings* as a sacrificial figure and as teaching the Æsir about *seiðr*, a kind of magic common among the Vanir. Soon after the contretemps with Gullveig, the Æsir are to be found in conclave, considering whether or not to share their sacrifices. The first war is inaugurated when they refuse, and Óðinn flings a spear over the Æsir forces, a gesture meant to make them invulnerable. But the

Vanir, like Gullveig, prove impossible to kill and so the two parties enter into negotiations. Hostages are exchanged, and the three Vanir, Njörðr and his children, come to live permanently among the gods. Hœnir and Mímir are sent to Vanaheimr, but their sojourn is not a success. Mímir always spoke up in councils, whereas Hœnir would simply say, 'Let others decide', if his companion were not present. The Vanir decided that they had had the worst of the exchange, beheaded Mímir and sent Hœnir back to the Æsir with the head. Óðinn treated the head with herbs which prevented decay, and with magic; thus it was able to speak to him and tell him about hidden things.

Hœnir (whose name, oddly, connects him with chickens) has, as we will see, limited further appearances in the extant mythology. Mímir's head seems to be associated with the Well beneath Yggdrasill, where Óðinn's eye is lodged, and the god consults the head from time to time. Other figures called Mímr or Hodd-mímir are named in the myths; whether they are versions of Mímir himself or are separate beings is unclear. Kvasir is also one of the Vanir and he too is involved in the hostage swap; his fate is described in the next

Óðinn hurls his spear over the Æsir before the battle against the Vanir commences, in order to confer invulnerability upon the gods.
Lorenz Frølich (1895).

Seiðr: Secret Rites

We know very little about *seiðr* as a set of magical practices. It may have been a form of spirit divination, associated with the Sámi (Lapps), the Scandinavians' northern neighbours. Loki's taunting of Óðinn that 'you beat on a drum as seeresses do' suggests Sámi-type ritual. Usually women perform *seiðr*; in *Eiríks saga rauða* (Erik the Red's Saga) a seeress, wearing a glass-bead necklace and catskin gloves, after a meal consisting mostly of animal hearts, sits on a special platform; aided by ritual chanting, she prophesies when the famine in that part of Greenland will end. Cross-dressing seems to be involved for male *seiðmenn*; this is particularly disreputable. An early Norwegian king thought nothing of drowning eighty such wizards by marooning them on a skerry (a low-lying group of rocks in the sea) for plotting against his life.

The *seiðmenn* drown on the skerry where King Haraldr Fairhair has sent them for execution. Halfdan Egedius (1899).

chapter. The remaining Vanir seem to accommodate themselves to their new surroundings, acquiring palaces and occupying a distinctive fertility niche among the divine functions. Njörðr is patron of seafarers and fishermen; the evidence is in the little verses recorded by Snorri to account for his and Skaði's marital breakdown:

Njörðr said:
I'm tired of the mountains
I wasn't there longer
than nine nights;
the howling of the wolf
seemed to me horrible
beside the song of the swan.

Skaði said:
I couldn't sleep
in the beds by the sea
for the clamour of birds;
that one woke me
every morning
coming from out at sea: the gull.

THE TRICKING OF GYLFI, CH. 23

Njörðr, crowned with seaweed, and Skaði, accompanied by her
favourite wolf, discuss their differences.
Friedrich Heine (1882).

The Vanir seem to be subject to discrimination with regard to whom they may marry. Freyja marries up, it seems; her husband is a shadowy figure, one of the Æsir named Óðr, perhaps a double of Óðinn. He went away on a long journey, and she wept tears of gold for him (a popular kenning in skaldic verse for 'gold' is *grátr Freyju*, 'Freyja's tears'). Freyr lacks a wife until he falls in love with the giantess Gerðr (see Chapter 3), and Njörðr manages only this unsatisfactory match with Skaði; Snorri tells us that after their separation, Skaði and Óðinn had a large number of sons together. One of these, Sæmingr, was the ancestor of Jarl Hákon, an important Norwegian ruler.

This chapter has established the world in which the gods live, the constraints under which they must function and the space through which they move. In the next chapter we'll meet those other important inhabitants of the Norse cosmos: the giants.

3

OPPOSING POWERS

Our image of the giant tends to be derived from European folklore: we picture them as extremely large, hulking and ugly, and none too bright. While some of the giants encountered in legend fit this folk-loric model, the giants of myth are a complex and variable group. Ymir must have been very large indeed if he could furnish the material for manufacturing the universe, but other giants are closer to human (or divine) scale; some indeed can change their size depending on circumstances. Nor should their intelligence be underestimated. Giants take precedence in the mythic universe and have reservoirs of wisdom which the gods are eager to tap. Moreover, they have cunning and duplicity, which they harness to pursue their longer-term aims; and it's not always the gods who come out on top in these tales.

There is a range of different kinds of giant – and terms for giant – in Old Norse. It's not clear, however, if the words systematically distinguish different types. *Þurs*, sometimes translated as 'ogre', is related to the Old English word *þyrs*, the type of fen-haunting, demonic, cannibal creature that we meet in the poem *Beowulf* in the form of Grendel; but these associations are not shared by Grendel's northern cousins. The boundary between 'troll' and 'giant' is a distinctly fuzzy one; certain giants have three or more heads and are clearly envisaged as hideous and undesirable. Some giantesses can be ugly, sexually voracious and sinister; they harass heroes and gods alike and Þórr has no compunction in smiting them with his hammer. In a boasting match with his disguised father Óðinn, Þórr recounts one of his exploits:

I was in the east and I fought against giants,
malicious women who roamed in the mountains;
great would be the giant race if they all survived;
there'd be no humans within Miðgarðr.
HÁRBARÐR'S SONG, V. 23

89

Þórr's population control, achieved by extermination whenever he can find giants, seems to be important; in myths his absence is often explained by his being away in the east battling against them.

Giants are not always so ugly or threatening. Some giant women, such as Skaði, are fierce, but capable of a degree of assimilation into divine society; her association with hunting and skiing may suggest connections with the far north of Norway and the Sámi (Lapps) who lived by hunting, trapping and reindeer herding in the northernmost regions. Skaði's giant Otherness may reflect the Otherness of the Sámi, whose culture was very different from the Norse and who traded with, and paid taxes to, their southern neighbours. Gerðr, the daughter of the giant Gymir, captures Freyr's heart with her beauty and radiance;

Þórr's Battle at Geirrøðr's House

One such battle is recorded, unusually, in a skaldic poem. Loki has flown into the giant Geirrøðr's territory, using the flying-cloak, and has been captured. In order to ransom himself, Loki promises to induce Þórr to come to Geirrøðr's home, without his hammer Mjöllnir or his belt of divine power – it's a trap. Fortunately Þórr and his servant Þjálfi stop off at the home of a giantess called Gríðr and the god borrows a spare magic belt, her staff and some iron gloves. The weather in the mountains is grim, the river rises and the travellers are nearly swept away. They realize that the rising river is caused by one of Geirrøðr's daughters urinating; Þórr throws a stone up at her and 'dams the river at its source', or so he quips. At Geirrøðr's, Þórr is accommodated in a guest-room, but when he makes himself comfortable on a chair, it rises towards the ceiling, threatening to crush him. Using Gríðr's magic staff for support, Þórr bears down on the chair. Not only does he save himself, he breaks the backs of the two giant daughters hiding beneath it. When Þórr is summoned into Geirrøðr's hall, the giant casts glowing red-hot molten metal at him, but with his handy iron gloves, Þórr catches the missile and throws it straight back, through a pillar behind which the giant is sheltering, and through the giant himself. Þórr triumphs once again.

Þórr crushes the backs of Geirrøðr's giant daughters, who were hiding beneath his chair. Ernst Hansen (1941).

the young god sees her from afar and falls into despondency until his anxious parents (Njörðr and Skaði, in the role of stepmother) send one of his intimates, Skírnir, to winkle out of him why he is moping. Skírnir, an indeterminate being, whose name means 'Shining one' and who seems to represent some element of Freyr's fertility function, is dispatched with Freyr's magic sword to woo the young woman on his lord's behalf. Gerðr offers the visitor a polite welcome, but is unimpressed by his suit. Offers of the magic ring Draupnir and of eleven apples (maybe identical with Iðunn's apples of eternal youth) have no effect, nor Skírnir's threat that he will do battle with Gerðr's father. Only when the messenger threatens her with a long and complex curse, activated by carving runes on a stick cut from the green wood, a curse which would condemn her to sterility, nymphomania, misery and horror – and having only a three-headed giant for a husband – does Gerðr relent. She agrees to grant Freyr a rendezvous in nine nights' time, and Skírnir rides home with the good news, only for the impatient Freyr to complain at having to wait so long.

Freyr gazes out from the high seat Hliðskjálf, seeking his beloved Gerðr, while his anxious father and stepmother, Njörðr and Skaði, consult behind him. Illustration by W. G. Collingwood for a 1908 translation of the *Poetic Edda*.

Snorri's version of this story tailors it into a little romance; Freyr catches sight of Gerðr from Óðinn's high seat Hliðskjálf, and there's a distinct suggestion that his passion is a punishment for his trespass into the divine leader's space. Gerðr is undeniably lovely: 'her arms shine and from them / all the sea and the air catch light'. Skírnir is briskly dispatched and soon returns with the lady's agreement; there is no mention of her resistance or of the curse. The story is recounted in *The Tricking of Gylfi* to explain why Freyr has no sword, with the implication that it was foolish to trade that symbol of warlike masculinity for a mere woman – a misjudgment which Loki echoes in his critique of all the gods in *Loki's Quarrel*. How will Freyr fight at *ragnarök*, Loki taunts him, now he's given away his sword for Gymir's daughter?

Whether Gerðr consented to marry Freyr and came, like Skaði, to live among the gods, or whether the precious sword was bartered simply for a night of sexual satisfaction, is not related here. Elsewhere, Gerðr is explicitly identified as Freyr's wife and they have a son, Fjölnir, ancestor of the Swedish kings. That both Njörðr and Freyr end up with partners who are giantesses, not goddesses, may, as mentioned above, be an indicator of their lower status in comparison with the Æsir. The myth of Freyr and Gerðr has consistently been interpreted as a nature or fertility myth; the god of growth and fecundity must couple with the earth (Gerðr's name means 'enclosed place, field' and is related to 'garðr' in Miðgarðr and Ásgarðr). If the land is to be productive, it must yield to the god's embrace and open itself up to his fructifying touch. Yet it's not clear why Gerðr as symbol for the earth *should* resist the god's fertilizing ray (Skírnir), nor why she should have to be coerced into submission. The conflicted gender politics of the myth open it up to other readings. For although giants are strongly affiliated to nature, to chaos, the way in which they chiefly signify is as the Other, the oppositional, the different. In that role they are incorporated within the world of the gods, not situated completely outside it. There's a lot of coming and going between the domains of the gods and the giants. The gods, like Norse kings or great land-holders, seek to impress their authority on those they see as subordinate: they command that the giants entertain their superiors at feasts and provide the gods with the various benefits that are sought from them.

The myth of Freyr and Gerðr, in particular the relationship between the Vanir god and the giant woman's kindred, has also been read as political; the superior social group seeks to forge an alliance with those lower in the hierarchy and the gift – importantly, not exchange – of a woman is meant to seal the relationship. But this interpretation does not really map onto the poem as we have it. Freyr has no interest in Gerðr's family, no strategic reason to ally himself with Gymir by taking his daughter to wife. Rather he is driven by desire, and the tactics his envoy uses (bribery, with gifts that Skírnir may not have the authority to offer; threats; and finally curses) are disturbingly violent. To me the story has always seemed to reflect alarmingly the politics of the patriarchy. The powerful man sees a woman he desires and – by displacing the coercion onto his servant – succeeds in getting what he wants, despite the woman's

Skírnir, bearing the magic sword, and Gerðr; Gerðr raises her hand defiantly, in apparent rejection of his overtures. Lorenz Frølich (1895).

refusal and her depiction as having independence and agency (she has authority over her father's gold and a mind of her own). It's perhaps not surprising, then, that Snorri offers a more conventionally romantic version.

ᛟ THE BATTLE FOR CULTURE ᛟ

During the Æsir–Vanir war, the walls of Ásgarðr suffered considerable damage. In the aftermath, a builder presents himself, offering to rebuild the stronghold walls and make them impregnable in three seasons (the typical Norse time-measurement is half a year). In exchange, he demands the sun, the moon and Freyja. The gods meet in conclave and successfully haggle him down to a period of a single winter, and he has to perform the work single-handed. The builder agrees, on the quite reasonable condition that he may have the help of his horse, and the bargain is concluded. Imagine the gods' horror, then, as builder and horse labour day and night and the walls

The Myth of the Master-Builder

This tale of the master-builder, the supernatural figure whose skills are coveted, but whose cost is impossibly high and who ends up cheated of his reward, is an international folk-tale; Snorri's version of it is an extremely early one. In folk tradition the story is usually a stand-alone; the audience is expected to sympathize with the clever contractor who ends up with something for nothing. Quite often the builder is the devil in disguise and his being cheated is not ethically problematic. Richard Wagner makes use of the tale in *Das Rheingold* (The Rhine-gold), the first part of his operatic cycle *Der Ring des Niblungen* (The Ring of the Nibelung). Wotan (the equivalent of Óðinn) has concluded a bargain with the giants Fafner and Fasolt to build Walhall, his new palace. He has agreed to give them Freia as a reward, but when the other gods protest he negotiates with the giants to give them the Rheingold instead and, finally, he has to part with the ring of the Nibelung, stolen from the dwarfish Alberich. Alberich has forsworn love in order to steal the gold that belongs to the Rhine-maidens, and Wotan's confiscation of the treasure, and of the cursed ring, is partly responsible for the tragedies that follow in the cycle – including the downfall of the gods themselves.

Fafner and Fasolt drag Freia away. Arthur Rackham (1910).

The mysterious master-builder and his horse, constructing the
walls of Ásgarðr. Robert Engels (1919).

rise rapidly about their domain! It seems clear when only three days
of winter are left that the heavenly bodies and Freyja will be lost,
unless someone can come up with a plan – and Loki, blamed for
persuading the gods to accept the original agreement, is threatened
with death if he can't find a way of disrupting the builder's schedule.
Loki turns himself into a mare, who entices the builder's helpful
stallion away with a whinny and a toss of her mane. Although the
builder pursues his horse all night long through the forest, the con-
struction timetable is fatally curtailed. At this the builder falls into
'giant-rage' and reveals his true identity. Despite the oaths of safety
which had been sworn to the builder, Þórr is summoned, and (on
the grounds that the builder is not who he purported to be) the god
annihilates the giant with his hammer. Eight months later Loki gives
birth to a foal: the eight-legged horse Sleipnir, who carries Óðinn
through all the worlds.

Óðinn rides his eight-legged horse, Sleipnir, towards a woman who offers
him a drinking horn, on the Tjängvide picture stone, Gotland.

Just as in Wagner's retelling, the Norse gods are guilty, for they
have sworn oaths to the builder, guaranteeing not only his reward
but also his immunity while the work is under way. That these oaths
are broken – on the grounds that the builder was a 'mountain-giant'
in disguise – is troubling. Snorri foregrounds the ethical issue, citing
a verse from *The Seeress's Prophecy*:

> *The oaths broke apart, words and promises,*
> *all the solemn pledges that had passed between them.*
> *Þórr alone struck a blow there, swollen with rage.*
> *He seldom sits still when he hears such a thing!*
> THE SEERESS'S PROPHECY, V. 26; THE TRICKING OF GYLFI, CH. 42

The gods are shown to be oath-breakers, opening up questions of moral culpability which resound through divine history.
Is it permissible to break solemn oaths to giants – even if this one
had disguised his identity? This sundering of a sworn oath marks
the beginning of the gods' corruption and leads inexorably, it has
been argued, to their downfall. This may be to assume too much

coherence and continuity between different myths, recorded in very different contexts, but certainly in *The Seeress's Prophecy*, as we'll see in Chapter 6, the events leading up to *ragnarök* are carefully selected and arranged in a sequence which strongly suggests cause and effect.

For the moment though, the gods have come out on top. The walls of Ásgarðr are not the only goods which the giants can provide and which the gods covet. The culturally central myth of the mead of poetry tells of another such treasure. Once again, the divine substance is produced through violence and transformation, and it passes through different parts of the mythic universe before coming into the possession of gods and men. At the time of the hostage exchange between the Æsir and the Vanir (Chapter 2), both parties spat into a cauldron and from the spittle was made a being named Kvasir. He was the wisest of beings and travelled around the world, teaching wisdom, until he was murdered by two nasty dwarfs. They fermented his blood with honey and made a powerful mead. When questioned by the gods about his disappearance, the cheeky dwarfs claimed that their cleverest member had suffocated on his own wisdom because no one was smart enough to be able to ask him questions.

Next, the murderous dwarfs invite a giant called Gillingr to go fishing with them, upturning the boat and drowning him. They also murder his widow, because they've had enough of her wailing for her husband, and it's left to Gillingr's brother Suttungr to get vengeance: rowing the dwarfs out to a skerry and threatening to maroon them there to drown in their turn. The dwarfs buy their lives with the blood-mead; Suttungr takes the precious liquid home, stores it in three huge vats and sets his daughter Gunnlöð to guard it. Óðinn evolves an elaborate plot to steal the mead; he comes to the home of Baugi, another of Suttungr's brothers, where his labourers are cutting the hay. He sharpens their scythes with a magic whetstone and, when they all express the desire to possess it, he hurls it up in the air. In the rush to seize it, they all cut off one another's heads. This allows the disguised Óðinn to take over their tasks, on condition that Baugi assist him in getting a drink of his brother's mead. At the end of his labours, Baugi comes with Óðinn to Suttungr's, but the reward is refused. With Baugi's grudging help, Óðinn bores a passage with an augur into the mountain Hnitbjörg (Clashing-rocks) where Gunnlöð and the mead are to be found, and changes himself into a serpent in order to wriggle inside. There he seduces Gunnlöð and sleeps three nights with her, after which he is permitted three drinks of the precious mead.

Óðinn drains each of the three vats to the dregs with each drink, changes himself into eagle form and flies away. Suttungr, perceiving himself robbed, pursues him also in eagle form. The Æsir prepare vats to catch the mead which Óðinn regurgitates once he is safely within the walls of Ásgarðr, but he excretes some of the mead backwards

Baugi and Óðinn drilling into the mountain with Rati, the augur,
to reach Gunnlöð and the mead of poetry. From an eighteenth-century
Icelandic manuscript.

into Suttungr's face in order to delay him. That mead falls outside the halls of the gods, and anyone can consume it; it is now said to be the inspiration of bad poets everywhere. Through his habitual trickery and readiness to break oaths while holding others to their promises, Óðinn gains a great boon for gods and men. This version is the only complete account of the winning of the mead of poetry, but a large number of kennings refer to poetry as the 'drink of dwarfs', the 'sea of Óðrerir' (the name of one of Suttungr's vats), or the 'booty of Óðinn', confirming the details of the myth.

The gods have the edge over the other denizens of the universe in this tale; the viciousness of the serial-killer dwarfs, the stupidity of Baugi's labourers and the gullibility of poor seduced Gunnlöð all validate the gods' appropriation of the mead. Better that poets

Gunnlöð is wooed by Óðinn, for a drink of the mead of poetry.
Lorenz Frølich (1895).

Óðinn in eagle-form excretes some mead backwards at the pursuing Suttungr.
From an eighteenth-century Icelandic manuscript.

Óðinn's Betrayal of Gunnlöð

In the poem *Sayings of the High One*, Óðinn boasts of this adventure.
Using the augur to bore his way into Suttungr's halls, risking his life,
he talks Gunnlöð into letting him drink the precious mead: 'a poor
reward I let her have in return / for her open-heartedness / for her
sorrowful spirit', he admits ruefully. Gunnlöð's beauty was cheaply
bought; she was seduced by the god, who may have promised to
betroth himself to her. The day after the theft, the frost-giants came to
Óðinn's hall to ask about what had happened; having 'sworn a sacred
ring-oath / how can his pledge be trusted?' Óðinn reckons that the lying
and Gunnlöð's heartbreak were all worth it, in order to bring the mead
of poetry back into the light. Gunnlöð doubtless feels differently.

should make use of it rather than its being hoarded in Suttungr's halls deep in the rocks. 'Use it or lose it' is a good watchword for cultural treasures; the poets who tell the mead-of-poetry tale are united in their belief that the inspirational draught is better off shared among them.

Another tale tells of the gods' acquisition of a mighty brewing cauldron from the giants. The gods order Ægir, ruler of the sea, to provide a great feast for them, behaviour which echoes the aristocratic and royal practices of Scandinavia. For kings and great lords would travel with their retinues to the homes of those who held land from them and expect to be feasted. This shared the burden of supporting the king's retinue among his nobles, using up their resources rather than his, and it also allowed the king to keep an eye on what the lords were up to: whether they were enforcing the law, properly collecting and passing on taxes, or whether they were plotting rebellion. So too the gods impose on Ægir the obligation to provide hospitality. To his objection that he has no cauldron sufficiently large to brew beer for them all, Týr ripostes that his father, the giant Hymir, possesses an enormous cauldron, and he and Þórr set off to the Giantlands to fetch it.

Týr and his giant-killing companion arrive at Hymir's home where Týr's mother, a beautiful woman 'all gold-decked ... with shining brows', welcomes them warmly, but expresses anxiety about her husband's reaction to his guests. Týr's grandmother (presumably on the paternal side), by contrast, has 900 heads. Once Hymir returns home, he declares that he'll lend the cauldron if either of his visitors can carry it away. This is a cue for various tests of strength. Týr's mother has warned the two gods to sit behind a pillar in the hall so that when her husband's shattering gaze is turned on them, it's the pillar and not they who are destroyed. After Þórr has eaten two whole oxen, Hymir takes him fishing to get further provisions; the story of the fishing-trip is related on page 105. Þórr's success provokes the giant to set up a further challenge: the god can take

Figure of Þórr from Eyrarland, Iceland.

the cauldron if he can smash the giant's goblet. Bashing it against the stone pillars in the hall results only in further damage to the building until Týr's mother reveals that Hymir's head is the hardest of all substances and the goblet is successfully destroyed. Þórr is allowed to carry off the cauldron, borne upside-down on his head so that the rings on its rim jingle at his heels. The two gods do not get far before they realize that Hymir and his cohorts are hurrying in pursuit. Turning to face them, Þórr destroys them all, and brings the cauldron home. The poem concludes in a triumphant tone: 'and the gods will drink in delight / ale at Ægir's every winter'. For the last feast hosted by Ægir, see Chapter 6.

The story of Hymir's cauldron fits the traditional pattern of the gods taking the objects that they need from the giants, for, from an Æsir perspective, they simply put the giant's cauldron to better

Þórr fishing for the Miðgarðs-serpent.
Johann Heinrich Füssli (1788).

use. There's a certain wistfulness about the giant's realization of his
successive losses: his goblet is smashed over his own head, his cauldron is confiscated, and his wife connives with her son and his
notorious giant-slaying companion to seize or destroy her husband's
treasured possessions. How Týr's mother comes to be married to a
giant – why he, the god associated with law and justice, should have
giant paternity – is unknown. It has been suggested that perhaps
Loki once occupied Týr's role in this story; if so, it wouldn't be the
only adventure in which Loki and Þórr team up, and Loki seems to
be of mixed Æsir–giant blood. Striking in this poem is the frosti-
ness of Hymir, who personifies the forces of winter. Icicles tinkle in

Þórr's Fishing Expedition

After Þórr has eaten his host out of house and home, Hymir decides that they will go fishing to replenish the food supplies. Provocatively, Þórr wrenches off the head of one of Hymir's bulls to use as bait. God and giant row out into the ocean, beyond the normal fishing-limits and, although he catches two whales, Hymir expresses his nervousness about fishing so far out. But Þórr has laid out his line and no less impressive a sea-creature than the Miðgarðs-serpent swallows his ox-head bait. The mighty monster is hauled out of the sea; god and serpent stare at one another in a cosmic stand-off. In some early poems, Þórr kills the Miðgarðs-serpent there and then, but other traditions demand that the creature survive to battle against the god at *ragnarök*. Picture-stones show how, in the titanic battle between the two, Þórr sometimes puts his foot right through the bottom of the boat as he grips the line where the monster is thrashing. Hymir is terrified by Þórr's bold fishing behaviour and, drawing a knife, cuts the line, so that the Miðgarðs-serpent sinks back into the depths. In Snorri's version of the story, Þórr boxes Hymir's ears so that he falls overboard and is drowned; the serpent meanwhile bides its time until *ragnarök*.

his beard when he comes in from hunting, and his chilly gaze shatters what lies in front of it. Only his wife's insistence on the laws of kinship and hospitality recall Hymir to observing the social norms as far as his son and guest are concerned, and there's a fair amount of comedy in the giant's horror at the way Þórr's prodigious appetite depletes their food-stocks.

Þórr in his turn delights in provoking his host; the same hospitality laws that constrain Hymir restrain him from killing the giant in his own home, but once the giant reneges on the agreement to give the cauldron to the one who can lift it, he's fair game for Mjöllnir. He and the other 'lava-whales' (his fellow giants) are speedily dispatched by Þórr.

Þjazi, in eagle form, prevents the gods' dinner from cooking.
From an eighteenth-century Icelandic manuscript.

⚔ RECOVERING STOLEN TREASURES ⚔

We saw above how the master-builder was thwarted in the nick of time from taking possession of the sun, moon and Freyja, almost plunging the world of gods and men into endless darkness. This is not the only counter-move in the battle for vital treasures that the gods and giants wage. On another occasion, Loki is taken captive by the giant Þjazi, Skaði's father. Three gods, Loki, Óðinn and the mysterious Hœnir, were away on a journey and they killed and began to cook an ox. But the meat would not cook, and after a while the baffled and hungry gods realized that up in the oak tree beneath which they were cooking sat an enormous eagle. He declared himself responsible for inhibiting the cooking process. Loki seized a great pole and struck at the eagle with it; the eagle flew off, but the pole,

Loki ushers the unsuspecting Iðunn towards the forest where
Þjazi waits to abduct her. John Bauer (1911).

and Loki with it, stuck to the bird. Loki was borne away, his shoul-
ders in severe danger of dislocation as he desperately clung on. To
save his life Loki agreed to the eagle's demand (for he was the giant
Þjazi in disguise): he would entice Iðunn out of Ásgarðr and into
the giant's power. By telling Iðunn that he had found some apples
which looked very much like hers out in the forest, and persuading her to bring the apples with her for the purpose of comparison,
Loki tricked Iðunn into leaving Ásgarðr with him. Þjazi swooped
down on her and flew away with her, apples and all.

Once again, having got the gods into trouble, Loki is charged
with sorting out the situation. For with Iðunn's loss, the gods no
longer have access to the apples of eternal youth and they begin to
age. A council-meeting reveals that Iðunn was last seen in Loki's
company; his complicity in her disappearance is proven. Wearing

Four queens from the Lewis chessmen. The pieces were made in the late twelfth century, probably in Scandinavia.

The Sleeping Army
The novelist Francesca Simon, author of the *Horrid Henry* stories, has written a novel, *The Sleeping Army* (2012), about a little girl called Freya who blows a Viking-Age horn lying next to the Lewis Chessmen in the British Museum. This precipitates her into the world of the gods. Freya has to assist Thor's two human helpers (here called Alfie and Roskva), and a smelly berserker warrior called Snot (Wise One) to rescue Iðunn and her apples of youth from the giants. Freya learns much about her capacities and does a fair bit of growing up in her race not only to save the gods from ageing, but also to prevent herself and her companions from turning into chessmen themselves, and joining other failed questers in the museum case – the Sleeping Army of the title.

Freyja's falcon-feather-cloak, Loki flies to Þjazi's hall where he takes advantage of the giant's absence out fishing to turn Iðunn into a nut. He makes off with her and her vital apples. When Þjazi discovers his loss, he pursues Loki in eagle form; the Æsir make a great pile of wood-shavings within the precincts of Ásgarðr and, while the exhausted Loki drops down with his burden just within the wall, the eagle is unable to stop and overflies his prey. The gods set fire to the wood-shavings and the eagle's feathers are soon ablaze. When he abandons his avian form, the gods swiftly kill him. Þjazi's death brings Skaði to Ásgarðr seeking compensation, with the consequences that we saw in Chapter 1. The gods resume their usual fruit diet and soon they are restored to their full vigour.

☒ DRAGGING ÞÓRR UP ☒

This mythic pattern, in which the giants seize hold of something crucial to the gods' wellbeing, is burlesqued in *Þrymskviða* (Þrymr's Poem). Þórr awakens one morning to find that his hammer Mjöllnir is missing; his beard bristles in alarm and he calls for Loki. For once, Loki is not behind the theft and he willingly borrows Freyja's feather-cloak and heads to the Giantlands. Here he encounters the giant Þrymr who is sitting on a grave-mound, plaiting leashes for his elegant hunting dogs and neatly trimming his horses' manes: this is clearly a giant with aristocratic pretensions. Þrymr readily admits that he has the hammer and states that he will return it only if he is given Freyja as his bride. Loki speeds home with the news and he and Þórr go to see Freyja. With a typical lack of subtlety they baldly announce to the goddess that she is to put on a bridal head-dress and get ready to drive to the Giantlands to be wed. Freyja does not take this news well:

> *Furious then was Freyja and snorted in rage,*
> *the whole hall of the Æsir trembled at that;*
> *the great neck-ring of the Brisings fell from her.*
> *'You'll know me to be the most man-mad of women*
> *if I drive with you to the land of the giants.'*
> ÞRYMR'S POEM, V. 13

Part of the joke, of course, is that Freyja *is* the 'most man-mad of women', but even she draws the line at marrying a giant. What to do? The gods meet in council, and Heimdallr comes up with the wonderful idea of dressing Þórr as a woman and sending him in Freyja's place. Þórr's strenuous objections go unheeded for, as Loki points out, unless the hammer is restored, the giants will soon be moving into Ásgarðr. And so Þórr is attired in women's clothes, complete with bridal head-dress, and a bunch of keys (symbolic of female authority within the home) hanging from his girdle. Freyja lends her neck-ring, the *Brisinga men*, as a final authentic touch. Loki too dons female dress and the pair set off in Þórr's goat-drawn chariot.

Þórr being dressed in women's clothes, in order to pose
as Freyja for the 'wedding' to Þrymr.
Elmer Boyd Smith (1902).

How Þórr Gained his Servants

Þórr's goats, Tanngrisnir and Tanngnjóstr (Tooth-grinder; Tooth-gnasher) are very useful animals. Not only do they draw the god's chariot, but when he is travelling, he can kill and eat them, and then, by laying their bones on their skins, revive them the next morning, ready for the onward journey. Once Þórr was staying with a poor man called Egill, who had no meat for supper. Þórr slaughtered the goats and shared the meat with the family, warning that no one should split the bones to get at the juicy marrow within. When the goats were reconstituted next morning, one was visibly limping, and Þórr furiously demanded who had disobeyed him. The son of the family, Þjálfi, owned up and the terrified father offered his two children to the god in recompense. Thus Þórr gained his two human servants, Þjálfi and his sister Röskva; Þjálfi appears in various adventures, but Röskva is little mentioned.

Meanwhile, in the Giantlands, Þrymr is quivering with excitement, ordering preparations to be made for the wedding-feast and bragging about his possessions:

> *Gold-horned cows walk here in the yard,*
> *jet-black oxen to the giant's delight;*
> *heaps I have of treasures, heaps I have of luxuries;*
> *only Freyja seemed to be missing.*
> ÞRYMR'S POEM, V. 23

A heavily veiled Freyja sits down to the feast and astonishes her bridegroom by consuming 'one whole ox, eight salmon / all the dainties meant for the women / ... [and] three casks of mead'. Loki, as bridesmaid, hastily explains that her mistress has not eaten for eight nights, so madly keen was she to come to the Giantlands. Þrymr thinks to steal a kiss from his bride, but when he peeps under the veil he is alarmed by the lady's fiery red eyes. Quick-thinking Loki explains that this is caused by sleeplessness in anticipation of the wedding. The giant's sister demands gifts from the bride, then the hammer is finally produced in order to sanctify the marriage – perhaps a reference to actual wedding rituals. As soon as Þórr has his hammer in his hand, he smashes the wheedling sister-in-law, and slaughters all the rest of the wedding guests before he and Loki set off home. Ásgarðr is safe once more and the hammer back with its rightful owner.

This tale may be a rather late one, given the lack of seriousness with which the gods are treated. Both Þórr and Freyja are undignified in their emotional responses. Þórr gropes around for his hammer before yelling for Loki; Freyja's snorting and her heaving bosom cause her favourite adornment to snap and fall from her – and we remember the high price that she paid the dwarfs for it (see Chapter 2). Þrymr's social pretensions are neatly skewered by his self-satisfaction – all he needed was the goddess of beauty and sex as his wife to complete his collection of valuables. The comedy of that most masculine of the gods being forced into women's clothing, and Loki's alacrity in offering to go along also in female dress, points on the one hand to the gender ambiguity that surrounds Loki and his shape-shifting, and on the other to the strong cultural taboos against cross-dressing and other transgender activities, particularly if undertaken in connection with the practice of *seiðr*. Óðinn is less sensitive in this regard; as we will see in Chapter 6, he is not above disguising himself as a woman, if circumstances demand it.

⚹ ÞÓRR'S VISIT TO ÚTGARÐA-LOKI ⚹

The most elaborate tale of Þórr's dealings with the giants is told at length by Snorri. Þórr and Loki set out one day to go adventuring in the goat-drawn chariot. This is when Þórr acquires his two human servants (see page 111), and later the next evening the party finds itself in a forest. Ahead is some kind of a hall so they seek shelter there, but in the middle of the night there's an earthquake and the alarmed party huddle in a smaller room just off the main hall. The next day when they come out of the hall they find a huge man lying snoring beside it – the source of the previous night's earthquake. Þórr is about to strike this figure with his hammer when he awakens. He recognizes the god, whom he greets by name, and asks, 'why did you drag off my glove?' The astonished travellers realize that the hall in which they spent the night was the giant's glove, while the side-room was the thumb. The giant, who calls himself Skrýmir, offers his companionship and they journey together. All their provisions are placed in a bag which Skrýmir carries; that evening Þórr proves unable to open it to get dinner while the giant takes a nap. So annoyed is the god that he strikes Skrýmir the mightiest blow he can muster with Mjöllnir. But the giant opens his eyes, mutters that a leaf must have fallen on him from the oak-tree under which he is snoozing, and enquires as to whether they've had their dinner. The humiliated god dissembles about their hunger and in the middle of the night he strikes the sleeping Skrýmir a second blow; a mere acorn, the giant claims when he's awakened by it. A third attack is no more successful.

The next day Skrýmir parts company with the divine party as they come to a giant-dwelling named Útgarðr; its lord is (also) called Loki, taking his byname from his home. Skrýmir warns his new friends not to be cheeky at Útgarða-Loki's place since they are mere babes-in-arms in comparison with the mighty men in the fortress. And the inhabitants of the hall are indeed impressively large. Útgarða-Loki welcomes his guests and invites them to take part in various competitions for general amusement. First up is Loki, who volunteers in an eating contest. Though he clears his trough of food in record time, his opponent Logi eats not only the food, and the bones, but also the trough itself. One-nil to the giants! Þjálfi runs a race against a certain Hugi; though the boy does well, over the best of three he's clearly the loser. Þórr's participation in a drinking

A tiny Þórr strikes the sleeping giant Skrýmir; his enormous glove
is in the foreground. Friedrich Heine (1882).

competition is also pitiful. He's challenged to drain a horn of liquid
which, apparently, can usually be drained by the feeblest drinker in
three draughts. But even after three lung-bursting gulps, the level in
the horn has only sunk a fraction. Now Útgarða-Loki expresses his
scorn by inviting the god to try two further exploits: picking up his
cat and wrestling with his old nurse. Alas, Þórr is no more impressive; he can only raise one paw of the cat from the ground, while
the nurse, Elli, manages to drop Þórr onto one knee. Thoroughly
embarrassed by their team's performance, Þórr and his friends
nevertheless enjoy the hospitality on offer, and, after an excellent
breakfast, they ready themselves to go home.

Útgarða-Loki accompanies them some distance from his stronghold and then reveals the truth of what's been going on; he'll never
be letting the mighty god back under his roof, so dangerous is he.
For Útgarða-Loki and Skrýmir are one and the same; the food-bag
was tied with magic wire; the sleeping giant had magically inter-
posed a mountain between his head and Þórr's hammer-blows, and

Þórr wrestles with Útgarða-Loki's cat.
Frederick Richardson (1913).

the evidence, a tabletop mountain, now with three square valleys in it, is visible some way off. As for the contest within Útgarðr itself, Loki had been pitched against Fire, who of course had no difficulty in consuming the food-trough; Þjálfi had raced against Thought, and the drinking-horn had been connected to the ocean. No wonder then that Þórr had not been able to drain it, though his efforts in lowering the level in the horn explain the existence of the tides. The black cat – well, that was none other than the mighty Miðgarðs-serpent itself, while Elli the nurse was Old Age, who brings every man to his knees sooner or later. Having imparted this information, Útgarða-Loki and his hall vanish, just as Þórr is raising Mjöllnir in order to annihilate him.

This tale, with its allegorical representation of Fire, Thought and Old Age, suggests that Snorri expanded on an earlier tale in which Þórr meets a cunning giant with an enormous glove. In *Loki's Quarrel* (see below), Loki twits the god with having cowered in the glove and with failing to open the food-bag; these elements at least must be traditional. One curious detail is Skrýmir's assumed name of Útgarða-Loki. Is he at some level a double of Loki? Does the cunning god divide himself between playing the brains to Þórr's brawn, and displaying a clear giant aspect, bent on defending the Giantlands against Þórr's readiness to lash out with his hammer? It's one thing to cheer Þórr killing all the giant wedding guests after Þrymr stole his hammer, or smashing Hymir and his troops when he reneged on the promise to let Þórr have the cauldron, or to hear at second hand of his slaughter of giants away in the east. But it's quite another to see him ready to murder a sleeping man who has sought only to embarrass, not to harm, him. Þórr's dignity is somewhat recuperated by the revelation that he has been matched against metaphysical forces. Yet, once he finds himself defeated by the ocean, by the cosmic monster who symbolizes the limits of geographical space and by Old Age, the most salient aspect of Time for us humans, he reacts with peevishness. This equivocal characterization of Þórr suggests that Snorri has re-drawn him in a less than flattering light, taking his cue from older tales.

☙ ÞÓRR VERSUS ÓÐINN ☙

One final insight into Þórr's role in the mythological system is offered in the lively poem *Hárbarðsljóð* (Hárbarðr's, or Grey-beard's, Song). Þórr is on his way home when he comes to a fjord. He hails the ferryman to ask for passage, not realizing that the old man with the boat is his own father, Óðinn, in disguise. To Þórr's astonishment the ferryman meets his proud boast, 'with Þórr you converse here!' with insults and counter-boasts. The two gods participate in a *flyting*, a formal exchange of claims to greatness, rebuttals and counter-claims. But where Þórr brags of killing giants, including Hrungnir and Skaði's father Þjazi, of smiting berserk women and giantesses, the ferryman's counter-claims are not of matching

heroic achievements. Rather, if he is telling the truth, Óðinn has
been busy seducing lovely women. 'How did it go with them?' Þórr
asks, sounding rather envious. Óðinn replies:

> *We had frisky women, if only they were well-disposed to us,*
> *we had clever women, if only they were faithful to us,*
> *they wound a rope out of sand*
> *and from a deep valley*
> *they dug out the ground;*
> *only I was superior to them with my shrewdness,*
> *I slept with the seven sisters*
> *and got all their hearts, and pleasure from them.*
> *What were you doing meanwhile, Þórr?*
> HÁRBARÐR'S SONG, V. 18

These mysterious women, described in riddling terms, seem to
be some sort of natural phenomenon, shaping the terrain in different ways. Þórr counters with the claim that he tossed Þjazi's eyes up
into the sky where they became a constellation, but his father remains
unimpressed. To each of Þórr's exploits, Óðinn replies with a boast
of having led an army (though he does not seem to fight in person),
of seducing women or of stirring up conflict – a traditional role for
the god which helps him to select the right personnel to join the
Einherjar. Þórr's bragging avails him nothing in the face of Óðinn's
indifference to claims to glory or honour. The senior god makes an
interesting assertion: 'Óðinn owns the nobles who fall in battle /
Þórr owns the race of thralls!' (v. 24). Þórr was the most popular god
in Iceland and Norway, perhaps because he ruled the weather, crucial
to those who live by the land or on the sea and those who labour
with their hands. Óðinn meanwhile is most closely associated with
aristocrats and poets, consequent on his role in winning the mead
of poetry for them; he is also a patron of kings. The poem ends with
Óðinn absolutely refusing to bring the ferry-boat over to Þórr and

The Duel between Þórr and Hrungnir

Hrungnir was a giant whom the gods ill-advisedly invited into Ásgarðr for a drink after he and Óðinn had been competing in a horse-race. The giant became drunk and began to boast that he'd dismantle Valhöll to take home to the Giantlands with him, destroy Ásgarðr and kill all the gods, except for Freyja and Sif whom he would take home too. When Þórr returned and found an intoxicated giant in Valhöll, he was enraged, but since Hrungnir was unarmed, they arranged to fight a duel elsewhere, at the borders of Hrungnir's own territory. Hrungnir had a heart made of stone, and a shield of the same substance; Hrungnir's ally was a giant figure made of clay called Mökkurkálfi, a bold enough being had he not been given a mare's heart – the only organ large enough to power his mighty frame. Þjálfi ran up to Hrungnir as he stood ready for battle and warned that Þórr was coming for him – underground! Hrungnir promptly stood on his stone shield, only to espy Þórr riding up in his chariot, surrounded by thunder and lightning. Hrungnir's weapon of choice was a whetstone, which he hurled at Þórr; the stone shattered in flight against Mjöllnir, and a fragment became embedded in Þórr's skull. Defenceless Hrungnir meanwhile fell to Þórr's hammer, toppling over so that his leg lay over the god's neck, trapping him. Þjálfi polished off Mökkurkálfi with little difficulty. But it proved impossible to shift the giant's body from the prostate Þórr, until along came Magni, Þórr's three-year-old son with the giantess Jarnsaxa. Magni easily heaved the limb off his trapped father, and regretted that he'd missed the fight, 'for I'd have had the giant away into Hel with my fists if I'd met him'. Getting the whetstone fragment out of Þórr's head was no easy task. Þórr asked a seeress to help sing the stone out, but as she was chanting he happened to mention that he'd given her husband Aurvandill a lift over the poisonous rivers to the north. His toe had frozen off in the cold and Þórr had tossed it up in the sky to become the morning-star. This news was so exciting that Gróa, the seeress, completely forgot her spells, and the stone fragment remains in Þórr's skull to this day.

claiming that he will find that his wife Sif is unfaithful to him. Þórr has to walk the long way round, despite his threats and bluster.

Many of the major myths, then, show giants and gods battling for possession over treasures which symbolize mastery over some aspect of culture. Mostly the gods come out on top, but the giants too have their victories and there's a disquieting sense that one day – the day of *ragnarök* – they will have the advantage. Loki is their inside man, occupying a strangely liminal space between gods and giants. His history (what we know of it) and his role, until the onset of the events heralding *ragnarök*, follows below.

☙ NEITHER ONE THING NOR THE OTHER ☙

Loki is a disturbing and tantalizing figure in the divine pantheon. There is no evidence that he was ever worshipped (the cunning choose Óðinn as their patron) and he does not give his name to farms, hills or other landscape features. He's said to be the son of Laufey and Fárbauti, a goddess and perhaps a giant. If his father were a giant it would explain both his transgressive nature (such relationships are normally forbidden) and his split loyalties. Loki is counted among the gods; he has sworn blood-brotherhood with Óðinn and, although he takes many oaths lightly, Óðinn never discounts this tie. Loki is among the Æsir early in their history, helping them wriggle out of the bargain with the master-builder, and setting out on journeys with Óðinn and Hœnir to see what is happening in the world. His impulsive behaviour on one such expedition, as seen above, led to his betrayal of Iðunn to Þjazi; in Chapter 4 we'll see how his casually shying a stone at a dozing otter triggers a long chain of disasters.

Loki's ambiguousness extends to shape-shifting and gender-bending. Mating with Svaðilfari, the master-builder's horse, caused him to give birth to Sleipnir, the best of horses. According to a mysterious sequence in *Hyndluljóð* (Hyndla's Song):

Loki ate some heart, roasted on a linden-wood fire,
a woman's thought-stone that he found half-singed;
Loptr was impregnated by a wicked woman,
from whom every ogress on earth is descended.
HYNDLA'S SONG, V. 41

Loptr is another name for Loki; here he becomes part of the genealogy of all the giantesses by perversely incorporating a female heart inside himself. *Hyndla's Song* is one of the few surviving poems to feature Freyja; she rides, apparently on her brother's golden boar, to visit the giantess Hyndla (Little Dog) to ask her a series of questions about origins and lineages. The boar-mount is in fact Freyja's protégé (and likely her lover) Óttarr, who needs to be able to recite his own lineage in order to claim his inheritance. Although Hyndla is reluctant to help Freyja (and exchanges some pithy insults with her), she warms to the task and imparts more information than Óttarr strictly needs – including Loki's pregnancy as the origin of ogresses. The poem ends with Hyndla's ill-natured cursing and Freyja's triumphant assertion that Óttarr now has enough information to contend against his rival, a certain Angantýr, for the inheritance.

⚥ LOKI'S CHILDREN ⚥

Loki has two sons by his wife Sigyn, variously named Váli (though that this son should share a name with Óðinn's late-born avenger of Baldr seems unlikely) or Nari and Narfi. Their fates are discussed in Chapter 6. Outside wedlock, however, he fathers three children with the giantess Angrboða. These are Fenrir the wolf, the Miðgarðs-serpent and Hel, the goddess of death. The monstrous offspring strike alarm into the gods. The Miðgarðs-serpent is cast out into the ocean where it lies with its tail in its mouth. Hel, with

The Miðgarðs-serpent, Fenrir and Hel: the children of Loki.
Willy Pogany (1920).

a face that is half corpse-blue, half a healthy human pink, is given the realm of Niflheimr (Mist-world) to rule over: the place where the unheroic dead (women, children and those who do not die in battle) go.

Fenrir the wolf is reared in Ásgarðr, but he is soon eating the gods out of house and home and it is decreed that he must be chained up. The gods cannot find a fetter strong enough to bind him, and after several failed attempts, which amuse Fenrir hugely, they make a pact with the dwarfs to make a magical chain. Forged from six things – some impossible: as a cat's footfall-sound, a woman's beard, a mountain's roots, a fish's breath; and some more ordinary: a bear's sinews and a bird's spittle – the bond was soft, silky and smooth. Fenrir smelled something fishy about this seemingly harmless ribbon and demanded a pledge that the gods would release him from the fetter if he could not break it. As the gods hesitated, Týr bravely stepped up to place his right hand in the beast's mouth. The fetter was wound about the wolf's paws and it hardened into iron as the beast struggled against it. Then, says Snorri, 'Everyone laughed – except Týr. He lost his hand.' Fenrir was imprisoned in a cave and a sword was stuck between upper and lower jaws as a prop so that his

Fenrir bound. From an eighteenth-century Icelandic manuscript.

Loki's Monstrous Offspring

Loki's children represent the metaphysical limitations of the created world. Fenrir figures the forces of Time; his kin lope through the sky in the tracks of the sun and moon, tongues lolling and jaws agape. On that great day, they will swallow up the heavenly bodies entirely. The Miðgarðs-serpent marks the outer edge of the known seas; also called the All-Lands-Girdler, it holds the world together within its closed circle. And Hel, the personification of Death, is, as we'll see later, a hospitable hostess, welcoming the dead to her hall from which they can never depart. She is the archetype of all those desiring and alluring female fate-figures whom we saw in Chapter 2, waiting to welcome men into their eternal embrace.

mouth must always gape open. Slaver runs from his jaws, forming one of the mighty rivers of the Other World, and there he waits for the end of Time, the coming of *ragnarök*.

There's more on Loki and his particular role in the events foreshadowing the end of the world in Chapter 6. In the next chapter we turn to some of the human heroes of Norse legend: the figures celebrated in the heroic poems in the second half of the Codex Regius collection. These are Völsungr, his son Sigmundr and his descendants, worthy inhabitants of Valhöll.

4

~~~~~~

FIT FOR VALHÖLL:
HUMAN HEROES

Of all the gods, it's Óðinn and Þórr who seem to be most frequently invoked by humans, at least in our surviving texts. Since heroic literature is largely composed for the social elite, it's not surprising that Óðinn figures in it largely as the ancestor of kings and the patron of heroes. The poem *Grímnismál* (Grímnir's Sayings) shows Óðinn delivering a bravura display of wisdom; he is tortured by being placed between two fires with neither food nor drink for eight nights. The king's son Agnarr offers him a horn of drink, an action that unleashes Óðinn's revelation of his identity and power. How did Óðinn come to be in this situation in the first place? The (probably much later) prose which prefaces the poem tells how Óðinn and Frigg fostered the two sons of King Hrauðungr. The boys had gone out fishing and drifted out of sight of land. They fetched up near

Frigg and Óðinn sitting in the high seat Hliðskjálf. Frigg scores points over Óðinn by claiming that his protégé, king Geirrøðr, is stingy to his guests.
Lorenz Frølich (1895).

a little farm. Here an old woman looked after Agnarr, the older, and an old man took care of younger Geirrøðr. Now these two figures were the gods in disguise, and come spring, the old man found a boat and sent the lads home, whispering something in Geirrøðr's ear before they said farewell. When they made land at their father's home, Geirrøðr was the first to leap ashore, giving the boat with his brother a smart push back out to sea with the words, 'Go where the troll will have you!' And out the boat went. Agnarr vanished.

Later when Óðinn and Frigg are sitting in the high seat Hliðskjálf, looking out over the worlds, Óðinn can't resist some point-scoring. 'Look!' he says, 'there's your fosterling raising children with an ogress in a cave. And there's my fosterling, ruling his kingdom.' Frigg retorts that Geirrøðr is a terrible king; he is so stingy with food that he tortures his guests if he thinks there are too many. This Óðinn must obviously investigate. Frigg sends Fulla, her servant, to Geirrøðr, to warn that a wizard is coming to visit him. Geirrøðr promptly seizes the visitor and has him tortured. At the end of Óðinn's mighty monologue, he finally reveals his identity:

The Terrible One will now take
the weapon-weary slaughtered man;
I know your life is over;
the dísir are against you, now you may see Óðinn,
draw near to me if you can!
GRÍMNIR'S SAYINGS, V. 53

In his haste to rescue his guest, Geirrøðr trips and falls onto his sword, and dies. Agnarr, the son named after Geirrøðr's betrayed brother, takes the throne.

As god of kingship, Óðinn needs to make sure that rulers fulfil the important obligations of hospitality. Yet his role in this little tale also acknowledges that deception and quick-thinking may be crucial in seizing the throne. Although the author of the prose passage insists that the charge against Geirrøðr was absolutely unjustified, and the god's ill-treatment was the result of Frigg's calumny, nevertheless Geirrøðr's torture of his guest – wizard or not – does call the king's judgment into question. It seems certain that Geirrøðr's trick on his brother was motivated by Óðinn, but that fate – or the intervention of the gods, playing their own private game – finally brings a second Agnarr to the throne. This Agnarr enjoys Óðinn's favour, for his giving of the horn of drink to the god is in effect a sacrifice, a tacit recognition of Óðinn's status, and Agnarr reigns for a long time after his father.

⚔ THE VÖLSUNG LINE AND THE FATAL SWORD ⚔

The dynasty whose history is this chapter's concern, the Völsungs, owe their very existence to Óðinn. According to the saga about them (probably composed around 1250), the earliest member of the lineage was a man called Sigi, said to be Óðinn's son. After murdering a thrall, Sigi was outlawed; Óðinn arranged for him to acquire some warships and Sigi took to raiding. He made his fortune, carved out a kingdom and got married. Eventually his brothers-in-law

---

The Magic Apple

Dynasties depend on reproductive success, and the wife of Rerir, Sigi's son, bore him no child. Frigg asked Óðinn to help them and he sent a valkyrie with a magic apple, immediately devoured by Rerir and (presumably) the queen. She became pregnant, but this state lasted for six years! The queen died, giving birth to a good-sized son by Caesarean section. This was Völsungr, who grew up to marry the very valkyrie who had overseen his conception. And Hljóð the valkyrie gave him no fewer than ten sons and a daughter. The youngest of the siblings were twins: a boy named Sigmundr and a girl, Signý.

Óðinn plunges the sword into the tree Barnstokkr in Völsungr's hall.
Emil Doepler (1905).

The Sword in the Tree

We recognize the mysterious stranger who plunges the sword into
the tree in Völsungr's hall as Óðinn. He is bestowing a gift on the next
generation of his descendants, to put a positive spin on this action.
Or else he has come to sow trouble, to find out which of the ten sons
of Völsungr is the one who is fit to carry forward the lineage. The tree's
centrality reminds us of the World-Tree Yggdrasill, growing up through
the centre of the worlds as Barnstokkr grows up through Völsungr's
hall. Its name, meaning 'Child-stock', underlines this part of the saga's
interest in genealogy, in the dynasty's progression from short-tempered
arrogant Sigi to Völsungr and his sons, from heroes who are born of
gods and valkyries through magic to more human champions, though
still conceived by somewhat aberrant means.

plotted against Sigi and murdered him while his son Rerir was away. Rerir returned and slew all those implicated in his father's death. Thus kin-murder and treachery became inscribed in the Völsung lineage from the very first.

Once his daughter Signý has grown up, Völsungr arranges a marriage for her with King Siggeirr of Gautland in southern Sweden. During the wedding-feast an elderly one-eyed man with a hat pulled down low over his eyes enters Völsungr's hall with a drawn sword in his hand. This he plunges into the great tree, Barnstokkr, which grows up in the middle of the hall, and the sword sinks in up to the hilt. The man announces that he who can pull the sword from the trunk may have it: no better sword will ever come into his hand.

Like the Sword in the Stone of Arthurian myth, this sword can only be pulled out by Óðinn's chosen; this proves to be Signý's brother Sigmundr. His new brother-in-law Siggeirr offers three times the sword's weight in gold for it, but Sigmundr refuses: if the sword were meant for Siggeirr it would have yielded to his tugging. Siggeirr lets this pass for now, but we sense trouble ahead. Not long afterwards comes a return invitation for Völsungr and his sons to visit Siggeirr and Signý in Gautland, but it's a trap. Siggeirr attacks his wife's kinsmen; Völsungr is killed and the brothers captured.

Desperately seeking a means to forestall her husband's execution of her brothers, Signý begs that they be placed in stocks and left out in the forest, while she tries to come up with a rescue plan. But on each successive night a huge she-wolf (some said Siggeirr's witch-mother transformed) comes and devours one of the brothers, until only Sigmundr is left. By now Signý has worked out what to do. She sends a servant to give her twin some honey; he smears this all over his face and waits for the she-wolf. Instead of savaging him, she begins to lick the honey from his face. Sigmundr seizes his chance; he opens his mouth and bites into the wolf's tongue, clamping on so firmly that the tongue is torn out. Writhing in agony, the she-wolf tears the stocks apart; as she dies, Sigmundr escapes into the depths of the forest.

Sigmundr, bound, bites the she-wolf's tongue. Willy Pogany (1920).

⚜ VENGEANCE, INCEST AND WEREWOLVES ⚜

As one man ranged against all Siggeirr's warriors, Sigmundr had no chance of taking vengeance. Signý had two sons by her hated husband, but her test of their mettle proved that they were too feeble to ally with their uncle and they were killed. Signý despaired of producing an adequate avenger. Exchanging her appearance with a wandering sorceress, she visited Sigmundr in his underground hideout and slept with him, while the sorceress remained with Siggeirr. Thus Signý gave birth to a child who was doubly a Völsung: Sinfjötli. He passed his mother and uncle's tests with ease and went to live with Sigmundr. So tough was Sinfjötli that he and his father even spent a period as were-wolves, after finding some shape-changing skins in the woods. But the pair fought in wolf-form and Sigmundr bit right through his son's throat. Had it not been for a magic leaf, brought to the sorrowing wolf-Sigmundr by a (doubtless Odinic) raven, that revived the dead Sinfjötli, the vengeance plan would have come to nothing.

Now the father and son felt ready for revenge and made their way to Siggeirr's hall. They hid behind some ale-barrels in an outer

The Testing of Sinfjötli

Before sending Sinfjötli to Sigmundr, Signý sewed him into his shirt, passing the needle through flesh and linen. Then she ripped the clothing from him and asked if it hurt. 'Grandfather Völsungr would not have thought that painful,' the boy proudly replied. Encouraged, Signý dispatched him to Sigmundr in his forest lair. Sigmundr handed him a bag of flour and asked him to make bread while he went out. On his return, Sinfjötli offered Sigmundr the loaf. Sigmundr refused to eat it, for there had been a poisonous snake within the bag. Sinfjötli had, so he said, noticed something moving but he had just kneaded it to death as he prepared the dough. While Signý's children by Siggeirr had taken fright at the wriggling object in the bag and failed to make any bread, Sinfjötli was clearly fierce enough to take on the vengeance for his murdered uncles and grandfather.

room, but one of Signý's two little children spotted them lurking there. Signý urged that they should be killed lest they give the game away; while tender-hearted Sigmundr couldn't bring himself to kill his sister's children, Sinfjötli had no such compunction. He killed both the little ones and threw them provocatively in front of Siggeirr. Captured and entombed in a huge mound, the two men broke out once again with Signý's help, and they promptly set Siggeirr's hall on fire. Signý revealed the truth of Sinfjötli's parentage, kissed her brother and son, and walked back into the fire. Her life's work, vengeance for her father and brothers, was complete, and she could not survive the stigma of her incest.

Finally Sigmundr returned to his ancestral lands with his strangely begotten son, where he married and had two further sons. Their history is related below. Sinfjötli makes a loyal companion and brother to his father's heir, but he eventually dies through his stepmother's treachery.

Sinfjötli's Death

Borghildr, Sigmundr's new wife, has a brother and he and Sinfjötli
compete for the same woman. There's a duel in which Borghildr's
brother is killed. Borghildr prepares a drinking-horn containing poison
and offers it to her stepson. Sinfjötli is wary, for the drink looks odd and
twice he voices his suspicions to his father. Sigmundr is so tough that
no poison can harm him. Impatiently he takes the horn and drinks it
off, suffering no ill effects. When a third horn is offered, Sinfjötli repeats
his doubts: 'This drink is cloudy, Dad!' Sigmundr retorts, 'Strain it
through your moustache, son!' And Sinfjötli drinks – and dies. Grief-
stricken Sigmundr carries his body away until he comes to a fjord.
A boatsman appears and offers passage across, but there is only room
for the corpse on board. The boatsman announces that Sigmundr must
walk round the fjord, pushes off and disappears for ever. This time
the boatsman needn't be described as aged and one-eyed for us
to recognize Óðinn, come to take Sinfjötli home to Valhöll.

Sigmundr hands the corpse of his son Sinfjötli over to the
mysterious boatsman. Johannes Gehrts (1901).

The valkyries, from an 1896 production of Richard Wagner's
opera, *Die Walküre*.

⚘ HELGI THE SACRED HERO ⚘

Embedded in the *Saga of the Völsungs*, and retold in two eddic
poems, is the tale of Helgi, Sigmundr's son by Borghildr. Helgi's
name means 'the sacred one', and he belongs to a recurrent legendary type: the hero who is the lover of a valkyrie (see page 33). This
tale has been grafted onto the Völsung cycle, for the sacred hero
must be fathered by someone and Sigmundr is as good a parent as
anyone. Helgi is, like Váli, Óðinn's son, precocious:

> *The son of Sigmundr stands in his mail-coat,*
> *one day old; now day has dawned!*
> *Sharp his eyes like fighters;*
> *he's the friend of wolves, we should be cheerful.*
> FIRST POEM OF HELGI, SLAYER OF HUNDINGR, V. 6

The Beasts of Battle
The beasts of battle are the raven, the eagle and the wolf. In Germanic tradition they have foreknowledge of when battles are in the offing and they make their way to the field of slaughter, greedily anticipating their gobbling up of the carrion. There's no higher praise in Old Norse poetry than to say of a king that he frequently gave the wolf breakfast.

So observes one raven to another, gleefully anticipating the corpses that this prodigious child will provide for the beasts of battle to feast on.

Helgi makes his name by killing a certain King Hundingr and many of his sons when he is only fifteen years old. On the way back from this victory, Helgi meets Sigrún, the beautiful valkyrie who loves him; she requests his help in dealing with Höðbroddr, the suitor to whom her father wishes to marry her: 'But, Helgi, I call Höðbroddr / a king as impressive as the kitten of a cat!', she adds. Helgi promises his aid, and despite dangerous seas described in stirring poetry, he makes land where Höðbroddr and his allies are waiting for him:

There was the splash of oars and the clash of iron,
shield smashed against shield, the Vikings rowed on;
hurtling beneath the nobles
surged the leader's ship far from the land.

Helgi ordered the high sail to be set,
his crew did not cringe at the meeting of the waves,
when Ægir's terrible daughter
wanted to capsize the stay-bridled wave-horse.

FIRST POEM OF HELGI, VV. 27, 29

A Viking-Age ship depicted on a picture-stone from
Tjängvide, Gotland.

Ægir's terrible daughter is a wave, and the 'stay-bridled wave-
horse', Helgi's longship. The battle ends with victory for Helgi and
he embraces an ecstatic Sigrún. The *First Poem of Helgi* ends here;
in the *Second Poem*, which relates the earlier part of the tale in more
detail, Sigrún seems more human. The valkyrie who rejoices in
slaughter recoils in horror when she learns that her father, and all
but one brother, have died so that she may choose her own husband.
Helgi makes peace with the surviving brother Dagr, but soon Dagr
sacrifices to Óðinn for vengeance; the god gives him a spear with
which he kills Helgi.

Helgi is not yet quite done with this life; a serving-maid
reports seeing the dead Helgi and his retinue riding into their
burial-mound. Sigrún is as overjoyed 'as the greedy hawks of
Óðinn / when they know of slaughter, steaming flesh', just like the
ravens who praised Helgi's prowess at his birth. Sigrún does not

quail from spending a final passionate night with her dead husband in the mound, kissing his bloody mouth and drinking fine liquors with him. Helgi reveals that her tears are disturbing him; her excessive grief is preventing his moving on into the next world. Come the dawn, Helgi and his men ride away to Valhöll, never to return. Sigrún may have learned to let her husband go, but sorrow and grief cause her death soon afterwards.

⚔ THE DRAGON-SLAYER SIGURÐR ⚔

Sinfjötli's death and the consequent breach with Borghildr leaves Sigmundr without an heir. Now well advanced in years he asks for the hand of Hjördís, the daughter of King Eylimi. A rival suitor, King Lyngvi, son of the Hundingr killed by Helgi, also presents himself. Offered a choice, Hjördís opts for the older and more renowned Sigmundr, and the marriage goes ahead. Lyngvi's response is to launch an invasion. Pregnant Hjördís and her servant take refuge in the woods as Sigmundr and her father join battle against the invaders. Despite his age, Sigmundr is undefeated until a one-eyed man in a broad-brimmed hat and dark cloak appears before him. He blocks Sigmundr's sword-stroke with his spear and the sword shatters. The tide of battle changes; Sigmundr and his father-in-law Eylimi fall.

Hjördís retrieves the sword-fragments from her dying husband and she is rescued from the battlefield by her husband's ally King Álfr. At his court she gives birth to Sigurðr, who is fostered by Reginn the smith. Reginn's covert aim is to use the young hero to retrieve the treasure guarded by Reginn's brother, Fáfnir the dragon. Sigurðr has his own set of priorities, however. His stepfather allows him to choose a horse from his stud; there Sigurðr meets a bearded man who advises him, and then reveals that the chosen horse Grani was sired by no less a beast than Óðinn's own Sleipnir. It's not long before Sigurðr emerges into heroic manhood. Reginn reforges Sigmundr's sword

Kirsten Flagstad as Brünnhilde in Wagner's *Die Walküre*, 1938.

Wagner's Version

In Wagner's *Die Walküre* (The Valkyrie), the second opera of the Ring Cycle, Siegmund and his sister Sieglinde have long been separated and she is unhappily wed to Hunding. When Siegmund, escaping his enemies, takes refuge in the couple's home, the brother and sister fall in love, even though they realize their relationship, and they make love. Next day, Siegmund must fight with Hunding and Wotan decrees that Siegmund will lose. Brünnhilde, Wotan's valkyrie daughter, is sent to make sure that this happens. But Brünnhilde takes pity on Siegmund and he is close to victory when Wotan suddenly appears and shatters his sword, Nothung, with a blow from his spear. Siegmund falls dead at Hunding's hands. Brünnhilde gathers the sword-fragments and Sieglinde to her and flees. Wotan punishes his errant daughter by stripping her of her divinity and decreeing that she must marry. Sieglinde, pregnant with the hero, Siegfried, takes refuge in the forest.

Reginn, left, and Sigurðr reforge Sigmundr's sword Gramr. A detail from the carved wooden doors of Hylestad church, Norway, *c.* 1200.

Gramr for him and Sigurðr mounts a naval expedition against Lyngvi in vengeance for his father. The campaign against Lyngvi is a great success and brings Sigurðr much renown. Now, at last, it's time for him to prove his mettle against the dragon.

Fáfnir Becomes a Dragon

Reginn and Fáfnir were brothers; their third brother Otr used to transform himself into an otter to catch fish. One day the three gods Loki, Óðinn and Hœnir came upon him and Loki threw a stone at Otr, killing him. The gods took the otter-skin and unwittingly showed it to Hreiðmarr, Otr's father, who promptly demanded recompense for his son. The gods obtained gold by capturing the dwarf Andvari and taking all he had, right down to a ring on which the furious dwarf laid a curse. And no sooner had Hreiðmarr accepted the treasure than his sons demanded a share, and Fáfnir killed his father for it. The curse was clearly working. Fáfnir then turned into a dragon and lay on the treasure-hoard, while Reginn plotted to get the gold for himself.

Sigurðr kills Fáfnir the dragon. A detail from the carved wooden
doors of Hylestad church, Norway, *c.* 1200.

Reginn leads Sigurðr up to the heath where the great serpent
lies on his heap of gold. Reginn advises the hero to dig a pit, lie
in it, and stab the dragon to the heart as he crawls down to the
river to drink, then he retreats out of harm's way. As Sigurðr sets to
digging, a bearded old man appears and advises him to dig several
pits so that the dragon's poisonous blood will run harmlessly away.
Then he vanishes. This is the last that Sigurðr will see of his family's patron; indeed it is Óðinn's last appearance in this legendary
cycle until the concluding deaths of Hamðir and Sörli, as we shall
see. Sigurðr's combat with Fáfnir is disappointingly undramatic; the
pit-ambush is successful and the dying dragon exchanges prophecies ('my brother will be the death of you, as he has been of me')
and wisdom with the young hero. Reginn emerges from his hiding-
place and orders Sigurðr to roast the dragon's heart over a fire while
he takes a nap. Sigurðr does as he's told; he prods the heart to see
if it's done and burns his finger. When he sucks it to ease the pain,
he finds that he can now understand the language of birds. A flock

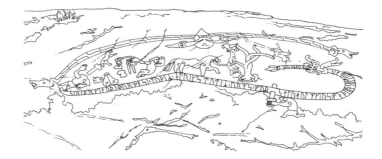

The Ramsund stone, Sweden, c. 1030. The rune-band forms the body of the
dragon, pierced from below by Sigurðr. Within the loop, from left to right,
the dead Reginn, Sigurðr tasting the dragon's blood, Grani the horse
and the talkative birds, perched on the tree.

Sigurðr on Picture-Stones

Sigurðr's adventures are frequently illustrated on Viking-Age stone
monuments. The best-known version is on the Swedish Ramsund
stone, which shows the story from the killing of Otr, via the killing of
the dragon (the rune-band through which Sigurðr is sticking his sword)
to the cooking of the heart, the birds' warning and the killing of Reginn.
There are other Swedish runestones with similar carvings, in varying
states of repair. Images of Sigurðr sticking his thumb in his mouth are
also quite common in British stone sculptures; there are images from
Ripon and Kirby Hall in Yorkshire. On the Isle of Man there are a
number of Sigurðr-related scenes carved on stone crosses. There's a
particularly good image on the stone labelled as Andreas 121, showing
Sigurðr roasting Fáfnir's heart (neatly sliced into rings) and putting his
finger in his mouth. The horse Grani is looking over his shoulder, ear
cocked to listen to the birds. Elsewhere in Man we see Sigurðr stabbing
the dragon; another stone shows both Loki shying the stone at Otr and
Grani with the gold on his back.

of nuthatches perched nearby warn him, as had Fáfnir, that Reginn plans to kill him for the gold. Sigurðr forestalls this by cutting off Reginn's head, loading Grani with the treasure and setting off for his next adventure: the encounter with the sleeping valkyrie on the mountain Hindarfjall.

Sigurðr roasts slices of Fáfnir's heart over the fire, while Grani looks over his shoulder. Detail from a Viking-Age stone cross, Andreas 121, Isle of Man.

Tolkien's Dragon

Smaug, J. R. R. Tolkien's dragon in *The Hobbit*, gets his name from an Old Norse word meaning 'crept'. He is based on Beowulf's dragon, a flying fire-breathing monster, but unlike the Old English dragon, and much more like Fáfnir, Smaug can talk. He has a long conversation with Bilbo the hobbit, who distracts him with a riddling conversation while he spies out the dragon's vulnerable spot, a place in his armpit where his scales have worn thin. This knowledge, imparted to Bard the Bowman by a friendly thrush, allows him to shoot the dragon down out of the skies. Bard is one of the Men of Dale, all of whom, like Sigurðr, understand the language of birds.

In the Old English poem *Beowulf*, which is much earlier than the saga and probably earlier than the eddic poems on which it's based, the dragon-fight is ascribed to Sigmundr, not his son, and it's a far more daring combat. Beowulf too participates in an epic struggle against a treasure-loving dragon who lurks in a barrow in his kingdom. Provoked by the theft of a single golden goblet, this dragon has wreaked fiery destruction over the land. Beowulf, aided by his young kinsman Wiglaf, kills the beast, saves his people and wins the hoard, but at the cost of his own life. Beowulf's dragon is a winged fire-drake and inherently more difficult to deal with than the crawling serpent Fáfnir; it must be trapped in its barrow and fought at close quarters, despite its fiery breath. The other great dragon-slayer of the north, Ragnarr Shaggy-breeches, whose tale is told in Chapter 5, uses cunning to overcome his monster and lives to tell the tale.

⚔ SIGURÐR AND THE VALKYRIE ⚔

Guided by his bird friends, and having eaten more of Fáfnir's heart, Sigurðr makes his way to Hindarfjall. There, surrounded by a shield-wall, sleeping in her mailshirt, lies a valkyrie. She had disobeyed Óðinn by giving victory to a handsome young prince instead of his elderly opponent and had been punished: Óðinn had pricked her with a sleep-thorn and decreed that she must marry. The young hero awakens the woman, who greets him warmly, offers him a 'memory-drink' and imparts magical and social wisdom to him. Here the Norse traditions become complicated. Eddic poems name the valkyrie as Sigrdrífa (Victory-procurer) and her counsels mark the point after which a whole section of the manuscript is missing. When the collection resumes, Sigurðr is already at the court of the Gjúkungs (see below) and enmeshed in the interlocking love-triangles set up by his brothers-in-law's deception. In the

Statue of Sigurðr (Siegfried) and Grani from the Siegfried fountain, Berlin, sculpted by Emil Cauer the Younger (1911).

Saga of the Völsungs, the valkyrie is named as Brynhildr; here she assumes the role of Sigrdrífa, whose function may simply have been to give vital advice to the hero.

Brynhildr clearly must have a valkyrie/shield-maiden element in her history, for in the saga, Sigurðr betrothes himself to her there on the mountain and rides on. Now, at least in the saga, the young man leaves the heroic–epic world behind and enters the sphere of courtly romance; a domain as rife with double-dealing as any of the king's halls from earlier in the cycle. Although he has pre-emptively killed his foster-father, Sigurðr is ill-equipped to deal with the kinds of politicking that he will now encounter.

Sigurðr comes to the court of the Gjúkungs at Worms on the Rhine. Here the brothers Gunnarr and Högni make him welcome and their mother Grímhildr plots to unite him to their family by

A Modern Reimagining of the Völsung Legend
The author Melvin Burgess has written two young adult novels based
on the Völsung legend. These are set in a cyberpunk future England
where genetic engineering is rife and rival ganglords tussle for control
over London. The first, *Bloodtide* (1999), is based on the story of
Sigmundr and Signý, while the second, *Bloodsong* (2005), follows
Sigurðr's fate: his quest to rescue Bryony, the equivalent of Brynhildr,
from the underground city where she is held captive and the double-
dealing on the part of his friends Gunar and Hogni. Burgess draws his
imagery from computer games, films and comic-books to create his
extraordinary vision. Both novels vividly reimagine the legends in ways
which engage with teenagers' struggles to find their identities and to
discover what they truly believe in.

marrying him to her daughter Guðrún. Guðrún herself quickly
falls in love with the handsome newcomer; Grímhildr gives Sigurðr
a magical 'drink of forgetting', and he is soon betrothed to Guðrún,
oblivious to his previous vows. Now Gunnarr decides to seek a
bride for himself and has heard tell of the shield-maiden Brynhildr,
dwelling in her hall surrounded by a flame-wall. She has sworn to
marry only the man who can pass through the flames. The young
men set out together, but Gunnarr's horse baulks at the fiery barrier.
Only Grani has the mettle to gallop through the inferno. Aided by
Grímhildr's magic, Gunnarr and Sigurðr exchange appearances and,
in Gunnarr's guise, Sigurðr crosses the flame-wall and spends three
nights with Brynhildr, laying his sword between them to ensure chas-
tity. Deeply unhappy, Brynhildr suspects that something is radically
amiss: surely only Sigurðr, her betrothed, could pass the flames? And
yet here, apparently, is Gunnarr, claiming her as his bride.

A double wedding is celebrated, during which the 'drink of forgetting' wears off for Sigurðr; he recalls his vows but decides to
remain silent. Brynhildr is both astonished and miserable at his

perfidy. When Guðrún and Brynhildr quarrel about precedence as they are washing at the river, Guðrún reveals the deception practised on her sister-in-law. Brynhildr shuts herself up in her quarters, plotting her vengeance. Neither Gunnarr nor Högni, nor yet a repentant Sigurðr, who offers to abandon Guðrún and marry her, can assuage Brynhildr's fury.

> *I shall have Sigurðr – or else he'll die—*
> *that young man I'll have in my arms.*

> *The words I'm speaking now I'll be sorry for later,*
> *Guðrún is his wife, and I am Gunnarr's;*
> *the hateful norns decreed this long torment for us. [...]*

> *I go without both happiness and husband,*
> *I'll pleasure myself with my savage thoughts.*
> SHORT POEM ABOUT SIGURÐR, VV. 6, 7, 9

Other complications are revealed in the eddic poems, once the sequence resumes after the missing leaves. Brynhildr has been bullied into marrying by her brother Atli, who has threatened to withhold her share of the parental inheritance if she refuses to wed. Reluctant to surrender her freedom, Brynhildr had herself devised the flame-wall test and sworn an oath to marry only the man who could cross it, an oath she has now been deceived into breaking. Brynhildr suggests to Gunnarr that Sigurðr was her 'first man', a claim that makes sense in terms of the earlier betrothal (and indeed in one tradition the pair have a daughter, see Chapter 5). Gunnarr construes this claim as Sigurðr having lied about the chaste nights he and Brynhildr spent together after the crossing of the flame-wall. Gunnarr does not want to lose Brynhildr nor her treasure, but she will not reconcile herself to him. His brother Högni heartily wishes that none of them had ever set eyes on Brynhildr. And Brynhildr herself wants Sigurðr dead.

Brünnhilde rides Grani into the flames at the end of *Götterdämmerung*.
Arthur Rackham (1911).

The domestic strife soon reaches crisis point; Gunnarr and Högni have sworn such strong oaths to Sigurðr that they fear to break them so they feed a potent magical brew to their youngest brother Guttormr, who had not sworn the oath, and Sigurðr is murdered. Different eddic poems suggest different locations for this; one says that the hero dies on the way to the Assembly, his death revealed by a riderless Grani who gallops home to Guðrún. Or he is killed in the forest, out hunting, as in the Middle High German *Nibelungenlied*. In the weightiest Old Norse tradition, Guttormr slays him as he lies in bed with Guðrún; she awakens to find herself bathed in her husband's blood. Guðrún is so traumatized that at first she cannot even weep, until her sister displays her husband's corpse to her. Brynhildr's rage remains unappeased; she curses the woman who has saved Guðrún's sanity. Guðrún seeks refuge in Denmark, away from the tumultuous aftermath of Sigurðr's death. Vengeance seems out of the question, for to kill her brothers for

Wagner's Brünnhilde and Siegfried

Wagner's Brünnhilde is awakened by the hero Siegfried in Act III of the third opera of the cycle, *Siegfried*, and the two look set for happiness together. But at the beginning of the final opera, *Götterdämmerung* (The Twilight of the Gods), Siegfried longs for further adventure and leaves his beloved, sailing off down the Rhine into the clutches of Gunther, Hagen (son of the Nibelung Alberich and Gunther's half-brother) and their sister Gutrune. The intrigue plays out as in the saga, with a 'drink of forgetting', an exchange of appearances, the deception of Brünnhilde and her reluctant marriage to Gunther. When Brünnhilde realizes what has happened, she reveals the secret of how Siegfried may be killed to Hagen, and Siegfried is murdered while they are hunting in the forest. Brünnhilde's decision to die on her beloved's funeral pyre precipitates the end of the gods' rule, but the cursed ring, which had passed from Siegfried to Brünnhilde and back to Siegfried again, is finally returned by Brünnhilde to the Rhine-maidens from whom it was first stolen.

plotting her husband's death would decimate her kindred and bring little satisfaction – and who is left to carry out that killing?

Brynhildr soon realizes that by causing Sigurðr's death she has left herself nothing to live for. She mounts his funeral pyre and prepares to die, delivering a long prophecy about the bleak future of the Gjúkungs. And so ends the Völsung line – for Sigurðr and Guðrún's little son Sigmundr was murdered along with his father. Brynhildr dies spectacularly. An eddic poem, *Helreið Brynhildar* (Brynhildr's Ride to Hel), shows her journeying after death to find Sigurðr. She passes the home of a giantess who reproaches her, 'It would befit you better to be at your weaving / than to be going to visit another woman's man'. Brynhildr, calling the giantess 'you very stupid woman', launches into self-vindication: 'the heirs of Gjúki made me love-bereft /and made me an oath-breaker'. And on she goes to her reunion with her beloved Sigurðr, never to be parted from him again.

⚥ GUÐRÚN AND ATLI ⚥

Brynhildr cannot forgive the bad faith of the Gjúkungs and her unwitting former lover, and exits the legend in a glorious blaze. Poor Guðrún, whose betrayal of her husband's secret has unleashed catastrophe, must find a way to continue. Despite the dire warnings that Brynhildr uttered in her final monologue, Guðrún's family are soon plotting to bring her home and marry her off again. Her new husband is Atli (Attila the Hun), Brynhildr's brother, who resents the family's treatment of his sister. The Gjúkungs owe him a woman, and Guðrún is sent to marry him. Again, traditions vary. In one poem they are said to have got on well at first, 'they lovingly / would embrace one another in front of the nobles'; in another they exchange recriminations about who behaved worse to whom, in a horrible display of marital wrangling. Atli and Guðrún have two sons, but the Huns' leader has his mind on seizing the treasure that belonged to his wife's former husband, now in the hands of her brothers.

Gunnarr in the snake-pit. A detail from the carved wooden doors of Hylestad church, Norway, *c.* 1200.

A friendly invitation to Gunnarr and Högni to visit (despite Guðrún's warnings that treachery underlies it) is accepted. In one poem, the brothers suspect that Atli means them no good, but regard it as cowardly to refuse to go; in another the messenger reveals the plot only when they are almost at Atli's farmhouse. The brothers fight desperately and are captured. Gunnarr refuses to reveal the whereabouts of the treasure unless he sees Högni's heart cut out from his body. After an attempt to substitute a slave's heart, Högni is killed: 'Then Högni laughed as they cut to his heart, / that living smith of scars, he never thought to cry out'. Gunnarr now knows that the secret will perish with him; he is cast into a snake-pit where, though he plays his harp to calm the serpents, one finally strikes him to the heart and he dies.

Meanwhile at home, Guðrún has taken terrible vengeance on her husband. When he returns from the snake-pit she welcomes him, offers him a drink, and provides snacks for him, and all the other Huns, to go with their ale. Only then does she reveal what they are eating:

> Your own sons' – sharer-out of swords –
> hearts, corpse-bloody, you are chewing up with honey;
> you are filling your stomach, proud lord, with dead human flesh,
> eating it as ale-appetisers and sending it to the high seat.
> POEM OF ATLI, V. 35

Guðrún has butchered their children and Atli has eaten them. In this poem she brings events to a speedy close, stabbing her drunken husband in bed, setting fire to the hall and going down to the seashore where she intends to drown herself. But the waves bear her away to the land of King Jónakr, where a third marriage awaits her.

In the other poem relating these events, Guðrún jests as she calls the boys to her, 'I've long wanted to cure you of old age'. The boys calmly accept their fate, warning, 'brief will be your respite from

---

'This Chain of Griefs'
Another, later poem reveals that Brynhildr had a sister, Oddrún, who loved Gunnarr 'as Brynhildr should have'. Once Brynhildr was dead, the tyrannical Atli refused to let Oddrún marry their sister's widower. Oddrún and Gunnarr became secret lovers until they were betrayed. Thus Atli had a double motive for the murder of his brother-in-law: family honour as well as withheld treasure. Both Guðrún and Oddrún share and give ready expression to the sorrow that is women's lot in this patriarchal and vengeance-oriented culture: 'to all ladies – may your sorrows grow less, / now this chain of griefs has been recounted', Guðrún concludes in her final utterance in eddic poetry.

---

rage / when you find out what results'. Guðrún's murder of her children, her forcing their father to take back into himself the sons who are flesh of his flesh, is a remarkably vivid sign of her rejection of the lineage into which she has been incorporated. The later parts of the Völsung–Gjúkung cycle develop the theme of the mistreatment of women, as mere objects of exchange between kin-groups, creatures whose feelings need be little regarded in the quest for political advantage through the forging of alliances.

⚔ GUÐRÚN'S VENGEANCE FOR HER DAUGHTER ⚔

The final movement of Guðrún's life sees her married to King Jónakr and mother to two more sons. Then tragedy strikes once again. For Guðrún and Sigurðr also had a daughter, it's now revealed, Svanhildr, 'the one of my children whom I loved best in my heart; / so was Svanhildr in my hall / like a splendidly glowing sun-ray'. Svanhildr is sent to wed Jörmunrekkr, King of the Goths. Jörmunrekkr's son by a previous marriage, Randvér, came to fetch his new stepmother, so close to him in age, and on the journey home they seem to have become friendly. Whether they fell in love, like Tristan and Isolde, whose story had begun to circulate in Scandinavia by the beginning of the thirteenth century, or whether the allegations against them were mere slander, is unclear. But Jörmunrekkr was persuaded that his honour had been impugned; he hanged his son and had his wife trampled to death by horses. From the scaffold Randvér sent him his own hawk with its feathers plucked out, and Jörmunrekkr quickly grasped the symbolism: he had crippled himself by executing his only heir. But this insight came too late; the hanging was already under way.

For Guðrún, the news that her last link with her dear Sigurðr, their daughter, has been killed in such a horrific way demands that Svanhildr be avenged on Jörmunrekkr. She summons her sons Hamðir and Sörli to her and, weeping, asks them to go on a mission of vengeance for their sister. The young men are reluctant – an attack on Jörmunrekkr in the Goths' stronghold is tantamount to suicide – and they remind their mother, when she compares their courage unfavourably with her brothers', how they triggered the cycle of vengeance-killing that she now seeks to perpetuate. Must a sister be avenged as a brother certainly would be? The question hangs in the air; killing women is rare in Norse legend and the ethics of the situation are uncertain. The story plays out across two poems. In one,

King Jörmunrekkr

Jörmunrekkr, a historical ruler over the Goths, seems to have been infamous for his tyrannical behaviour, for he appears in the Old English poem *Deor* (which, as mentioned in Chapter 2, also tells the story of Weland the Smith). Ermanric, as he's called in Old English, has a 'wolfish mind'. 'Þæt wæs grim cyning!' (that was a grim king!), the poet tells us, and many a warrior fervently wished that the kingdom might be overthrown and Ermanric deposed. And indeed, in Old Norse at least, he meets a well-deserved and horrible end.

the sons ride away on their mission, leaving their mother behind to mourn for them along with her other lost kindred, and to call for the building of a great oak-wood funeral pyre. For now she is ready to depart this world and be reunited with her beloved Sigurðr: 'Bridle, Sigurðr, the dark-coloured, shining horse, / the swift-footed charger – let it gallop here,' she commands.

In the other poem, Hamðir and Sörli set out in fury, goaded by their mother into seeking vengeance for Svanhildr. On their way from their father's court they meet their half-brother who riddlingly offers them assistance, 'as one foot does another'. Erpr, the half-brother, is metaphorically suggesting that kinsmen are all parts of the same body, but the other two wilfully refuse to decode his meaning and strike him down where he stands. Against all expectation, they enter the Goths' hall and capture Jörmunrekkr, cutting off his hands and feet and casting them into the fire. But the king has the wit to cry out to his men (for he realizes that the brothers are magically invulnerable), 'Stone them!' and his warriors obey. In the *Saga of the Völsungs*, the command to stone the brothers comes, inevitably, from a mysterious one-eyed old man who suddenly enters the hall. At last realizing their folly in killing Erpr ('Off his head would be now if Erpr were alive') the brothers die, congratulating themselves for having fought well, and comparing themselves to eagles, beasts of battle who perch on piles of the slain. At last the cycle of killings and vengeance is played out. There are no more Gjúkungs or Völsungs left.

The long Völsung / Gjúkung cycle is the best-known and most influential sequence of heroic legends from the north, thanks to Richard Wagner's operas and William Morris's epic poem, *The Story of Sigurd the Volsung and the Fall of the Niblungs*, which was published in 1876, the same year that Wagner's Ring-Cycle made its debut in Bayreuth. But there are a good number of other heroes whose stories are preserved in Norse legend, heroes whose ethics often made them challenging to write about. We'll meet them in the next chapter.

5

~~~~~~

HEROES OF THE
VIKING WORLD

The last chapter showed how the catastrophic dynastic history of the Völsungs and the Gjúkungs was retold in a sequence of poems, which explored the ethics of heroic behaviour and all that it entails: the over-valuing of masculine kinship and friendship networks against women's sense of their own selfhood, the problematic nature of vengeance, and the extraordinary allure of treasure. All these define the kind of Norse heroism that was inherited from Germanic tradition. There's little sense of altruism, of saving the community by fighting monsters, battling against invading armies or giving women freedom to make their own choices. The downfall of the Völsungs and the Gjúkungs is a salutary reminder that there is more to the heroic life than a prickly sense of your own honour. In this chapter we'll learn about a number of less well-known Norse champions and their different understandings of what makes a hero.

⚡ STARKAÐR THE STRONG ⚡

Starkaðr had a difficult heritage; his grandfather was a giant who abducted a princess, and his father Stórvirkr was born bigger and stronger than most men. Stórvirkr ran off with Unnr, the daughter of the Jarl of Hálogaland in northern Norway, against her family's wishes. Unnr's brothers pursued them to the island where they were living and burned the household alive. Somehow little Starkaðr escaped and was taken in by King Haraldr of Agde in southern Norway. Haraldr was later murdered by the king of Hordaland (where Bergen now is), and the three-year-old Starkaðr was fostered by a man with the odd name of Hrosshárs-Grani (Horse-hair-Grani, echoing the name of Sigurðr's remarkable horse). Nine years later, Haraldr's son Víkarr came looking for vengeance for his father, and found Starkaðr at Hrosshárs-Grani's. The young Starkaðr was

Coal-Biters

Coal-biters are unpromising, lazy boys who get their name from lying around in front of the fire and refusing to do anything useful. Often they are silent and sullen. They tend to annoy their fathers very much indeed, while their mothers often defend them, arguing that the idle lout will come good in the end. A good many Old Norse heroes start life in this way; a classic example is Offa of Angeln (northern Germany), in Saxo's account of him. He was silent as a youth and his father Wermund had him down as a simpleton. Then Wermund went blind, and the neighbouring Saxons threatened to invade. Wermund offered to fight their king in a duel, but they claimed that fighting a blind man was dishonourable. This spurred Offa into action. He fought against two Saxon champions at once, but his swords kept breaking because of his great strength. Wermund quickly had his old sword dug up – he'd abandoned it when he lost his sight – and given to his son, and with this weapon (with the unlikely-sounding name of Skræp), Offa won victory and honour among the Angles. J. R. R. Tolkien founded a 'Coalbiter' society in Oxford in 1926 – in fact an Old Norse reading group – and the name persisted long after his day.

a seemingly worthless 'coal-biter'. But he was also extremely large, dark-complexioned – and already had a beard at the age of twelve!

Víkarr gave Starkaðr weapons and took him off on his ship to seek out his father's killer. The king of Hordaland and his warriors put up a strong fight, but the foster-brothers prevailed. Starkaðr was horribly injured:

He [Starkaðr's opponent] hacked me painfully
with his sharp-edged sword against my shield,
sliced the helmet from my head, slashed into my skull;
my jawbone was cloven to the back-teeth,
and my left collar-bone ruined.
VÍKARR'S FRAGMENT, V. 14

Nevertheless he survived and for fifteen years he was Víkarr's dearest friend and right-hand man, in peace and war. Nothing lasts for ever, though, and one raiding season, Víkarr decided to head back to Hordaland to do some fighting. The fleet got only contrary winds and when they cast wooden slips to divine why, it became apparent that Óðinn wanted a sacrifice: someone must be hanged. And, shockingly, the lot fell on King Víkarr. Everyone went very quiet and they decided to have a meeting the next day to discuss this.

In the middle of the night, who should show up in the camp but Hросshárs-Grani? He quietly awakened his fosterling Starkaðr and rowed him over the water to a little wooded island. Twelve chairs were set up in a circle in a clearing; eleven were occupied and Hросshárs-Grani himself took the twelfth. The others greeted him as Óðinn and he announced that they had assembled to judge Starkaðr's fate. Þórr, one of those present, had it in for Starkaðr, for the girl who had run off with his grandfather had earlier turned down Þórr as a suitor, preferring a giant – and we know how Þórr feels about giants. The god proclaimed that Starkaðr should have no offspring. Óðinn played the part of the good fairy-godmother, decreeing that Starkaðr should live for three human lifetimes. 'And he'll do a dastardly deed in each of them,' announced Þórr. The competition between the gods continued. While Óðinn declared that his fosterling would have the best clothing and weapons, lots of treasure, victory in battle, the gift of poetic skill and would be honoured by all, Þórr countered with curses: Starkaðr would have neither house nor land, he'd be a miser, never thinking his treasure enough; he would be injured in every battle, unable to remember the poems that he composed, and though he might be highly honoured by nobles, he would be horrible to, and hated by, the common folk. The divine collective agreed to this fate for Starkaðr and he was rowed back to the camp. Hросshárs-Grani asked for a reward for the night's work and Starkaðr agreed. 'Give me the king,' said the old man, and he handed Starkaðr a spear disguised to look like a reed.

Next day, at the council, Starkaðr came up with a plan. They should carry out a mock-sacrifice of the king. He identified a tree with a low-hanging branch, and a tree stump was placed beneath it. A calf was killed and its guts twisted into a noose. Víkarr agreed that there could be no possible danger in standing on the stump with the noose, dangling from the low branch, just loosely laid around his neck. And so he stood there and Starkaðr jabbed at him with the reed in his hand, saying 'Now I give you to Óðinn!' But as he stabbed at Víkarr, the noose tightened around the king's neck, the tree branch sprang upwards, the stump on which the king stood rolled away – and the harmless reed became a spear. Pierced through and hanged, Víkarr died as an Odinic sacrifice. One more hero for Valhöll, but Starkaðr was driven away into exile.

That deed counted as one lifetime's worth of villainy for Starkaðr. Elsewhere we learn that, doubtless because of his giant ancestry, he was born with four extra arms. These Þórr obligingly tore off him, so that he looked a bit more human. After Víkarr's death, Starkaðr went raiding in various lands, where he achieved remarkable victories. He developed a striking hatred for actors and other entertainers; he left Uppsala, where he was present during one of the great sacrifices, because he couldn't abide the 'womanish body movements' of the participants and in Ireland he had a band of actors and singers thoroughly flogged. Although he had been in the service of the Danish crown, after the murder of King Frodi of Denmark Starkaðr left his son's court, disgusted by young King Ingeld's self-indulgence, and journeyed far and wide.

He returned to Denmark in the nick of time; Ingeld's younger sister was promised to a Norwegian, Helgi, but a band of savage warrior brothers, led by Angantýr (about whom more below), challenged Helgi for the hand of the bride. Starkaðr agreed to meet them in single combat and killed all of them, though he was left severely wounded, his bowels hanging out of a huge gash. Starkaðr propped himself up on a rock. A man driving a cart stopped and offered to help him for a reward, but Starkaðr decided that this man was too low-born and simply insulted him – showing the contempt for ordinary folk that Þórr had visited upon him. Another saviour appeared, but when the injured hero questioned him, this man admitted he had married a maidservant. This too disqualified him. A slave-woman was also rebuffed; finally a free-born farmer was permitted to bind up Starkaðr's stomach and stuff his guts back inside him.

Starkaðr returned to Ingeld's court, but was appalled to find that Ingeld's German wife had introduced interesting European cuisine (meat with sauces!), cushions, musicians (a particular *bête noire* as we know), witty conversation and decorated wine-goblets. Worst of all, Ingeld had forgiven and promoted the men who had murdered his father. Starkaðr lashed out in a long poem at all the decadent practices he saw around him; one which Saxo Grammaticus quotes at length and in Latin. This had the desired effect; Ingeld leapt to his feet, drew his sword and slew his father's murderers on the spot. The queen, with her fancy ways, was swiftly divorced.

After many more battles, Starkaðr was so worn out that he didn't want to live any longer, and he thought it would be unheroic to die of old age. He wandered the country trying to find someone who

The ageing Starkaðr offers a bag of gold to Hather, in order
to persuade the younger man to kill him.
Olaus Magnus (1555).

would kill him, with a bag of gold slung round his neck to reward his slayer. After (in line with his class views) rejecting a peasant's offer to kill him, he met Hather, the son of one of the many men he'd killed. Hather was ready to act, both in vengeance for his father and in hopes of the fee. The old man urged his opponent to strike off his head, and to run between head and body as the head flew off, for this would make Hather magically proof against any weapon. Hather indeed sliced off the head, but didn't risk running between head and body. Starkaðr's head flew through the air, gnashing its teeth and lodging itself deep in a tussock. The advice was nothing but a trick: had Hather come anywhere near the body, its toppling weight would have killed him outright. Starkaðr was buried with due honour in a barrow at that very spot. Þórr is blamed for Starkaðr's behaviour, but his decision to betray his friend Víkarr inaugurates a career of uncompromising violence, divorced from any understanding of ethics or helping others. His style of heroism alienates him from everyone around him: a warning about the effects of exaggerated masculine violence and the obsession with honour.

⚔ RAGNARR SHAGGY-BREECHES — THE OTHER DRAGON-SLAYER ⚔

The earl of Gautland in southern Sweden loved his daughter Þóra so much he decided to give her a little shining snake that he'd found. Þóra asked what would make it grow, and it turned out that placing a new golden coin underneath it every day was the answer – for, as we know, Germanic dragons are extremely fond of treasure. Before too long, the serpent was enormous, sitting on a huge pile of gold and eating a whole ox every day. He had entwined himself around Þóra's quarters and was friendly to her, but hostile to everyone else. This monster needed to be dealt with, and so the king advertised that whoever could kill it would have his daughter's hand – and the hoard as a dowry. No one dared face the creature, until young Ragnarr, son of the king of Denmark, heard tell of the serpent and the prize. He got ready a cloak and a pair of trousers made of shaggy fleece, and had them dipped in pitch. Then he sailed over to Gautland.

Ragnarr's weapon was a spear and he removed one of the nails securing the head. Then, after rolling in sand which glued itself nicely to the pitch, he boldly attacked the monster. He stabbed it with the spear; as the beast writhed in its death throes the loosened spear-head became stuck in its body. Ragnarr quickly turned away in retreat as a huge wave of poisonous blood erupted from the monster; thanks to his shaggy and sandy suit, he was unharmed. When he went to the earl's court to claim his reward, he was able to prove he was the dragon-slayer by showing how his spear-shaft fitted the head embedded in the monster's corpse, and he won Þóra's hand. A splendid feast was held and they were married. The couple had two brave and heroic sons, but then Þóra took ill and died. Ragnarr was so devastated by her death that he left his kingdom and sailed the seas, raiding and ravaging.

☙ A NEW WIFE — AND A NEW SET OF SONS ☙

Before their disastrous marriages to other people (see Chapter 4), Brynhildr and Sigurðr managed to have a daughter, little Áslaug, or so *Ragnarr's Saga* tells us. When Brynhildr went off to marry Gunnarr, she left her toddler with her foster-father Heimir. After the news of the terrible events at the Gjúkung court came to Heimir, he set off with Áslaug and a good supply of gold, both concealed in the case of his harp. He ended up being murdered by greedy Norwegian peasants, who stole the gold and raised Áslaug as their own, dirtying her face to hide her beauty and to stop her giving herself airs.

When Áslaug was grown up, the crew of Ragnarr Shaggy-breeches' ship happened to put in nearby for supplies, and despite

Áslaug's disguise, they perceived how lovely she was and reported back to Ragnarr. He promptly sent for her, commanding her to appear before him and setting her riddling conditions. Clever Áslaug could see this was her chance to escape from her cruel foster-parents, and, fulfilling Ragnarr's riddling conditions, she came to his longship. The king promptly offered to marry her, and indeed he made good on his word. On the wedding night, Áslaug strongly suggested to her new husband that they should wait three nights to consummate the marriage, for it was not auspicious to conceive that night. But Ragnarr took no notice of her request – and as a result, their first son Ívarr was born with cartilage instead of bones. He was unable to walk or fight, and so became known thereafter as Ívarr the Boneless. After that, Ragnarr took a little more notice of his wife's advice, and they soon had a fine crop of sons.

Ragnarr didn't know, however, that his wife was not really the daughter of the odious Norwegian peasants. After a while he decided that it might be strategic to marry the daughter of the Swedish king. He went off to Uppsala a-wooing and the match was on the verge of being settled when three birds, who had heard what was going on, flew to Denmark and reported Ragnarr's double-dealing to his wife – who had inherited her father's capacity to understand the speech of birds. When Ragnarr returned, nerving himself up to tell Áslaug about his plans, she made clear to him both that she knew what he was up to, and that she was the daughter of the most famous hero of the north, Sigurðr the Dragon-Slayer. To prove the truth of her words, the son that she was carrying would be born with snake-shaped pupils, emblematic of his grandfather's greatest feat. And so the baby, named Sigurðr Snake-in-the-Eye, came into the world, and no more was heard of Ragnarr's plans to marry again.

The king of Sweden was annoyed, both by his daughter's disap-pointment, and by the fact that Ragnarr's two eldest sons by his first wife, Þóra, came harrying in Sweden, and he captured and killed them both. When the news came back to Denmark, it was Áslaug,

Áslaug, clad in her fishing-net, with her canine companion,
ready to appear before Ragnarr Shaggy-breeches.
Mårten Eskil Winge (engraving of 1862 painting).

Ragnarr's Riddle Solved

Ragnarr decreed that Áslaug should come to him 'neither clothed nor
naked, neither fasting nor having eaten, neither alone nor with another
person'. Being a smart girl, Áslaug draped a fishing-net around her
body and let her hair hang loose, licked an onion so that her breath
was scented with it, and took the family dog down to the ship with
her. Ragnarr was impressed by her acumen and granted her the safe-
conduct she asked for. When the dog bit one of the sailors, they
strangled him with a bow-string, an early indication that Ragnarr
wouldn't always keep his promises.

A Magical Cow

The Swedes' secret weapon was a magical cow called Síbilja, whose
name means 'Eternal-bellower'. Her magical power was nourished
by sacrifice; when she was sent into battle her bellowing induced such
panic among the enemy army that they fought among themselves.
Síbilja also gored men with her horns. Counter-strategies such as
making enough noise in battle to drown out the bellowing didn't work
well, but, in a triumphant climax, Ívarr shot Síbilja through the eye,
and she dropped head-first. Then Ívarr catapulted himself on top of
her, magically increasing his weight and breaking her back. In a final
gesture, he tore off her head. The Swedes, naturally, fled.

their stepmother, who rallied her own sons, urging them that vengeance must be taken for their slain half-brothers, and who led the
seaborne invading forces. Ívarr the Boneless was the campaign's chief
strategist, despite his disability. Carried on a shield borne up on four
spear-points he commanded the warriors and gained the victory.

The sons of Ragnarr successfully ravaged England, raided widely
across Europe and were all set to attack Rome, a feat thwarted only by
a clever cobbler who used his sack of shoes meant for repair. 'Look!' he
said, emptying his sack. 'I wore out all these shoes just coming from
Rome.' This well-known folkloric ruse persuaded the brothers that
Rome was far too far away to be worth the trouble. Ragnarr himself
undertook a last ill-fated raid on England, against his wife's advice.
He was captured by King Ella of Northumbria, who hurled him into
his snake-pit. Despite the king's recitation of a long poem about his
many feats, the serpents finally struck to his heart. The snakes thus got
him in the end, ironically recalling his first mighty adventure.

When a messenger brought news of Ragnarr's shameful death
to his sons – and his wife – none of them seemed to react. But the
son playing chequers squeezed his gaming-piece so hard that blood
spurted from under his nails, the one shaving down the shaft of his

Ragnarr perishes in King Ella's snake-pit.
A French wood-engraving (c. 1860).

spear sliced a chunk of flesh from his finger, and another who was grip-
ping his spear left his hand-print in the wood before the spear snapped
in two. Ívarr's complexion turned from white to red to black in quick
succession. The messenger reported this to King Ella, who knew that
the brothers' apparent calm was misleading. Sure enough, they soon
came raiding in England and sought Ella out. At first it looked as if
the matter could be settled by compensation; Ella granted Ívarr some
land, but through the well-known trick of cutting up an ox-hide
into thin strips and claiming all the land that could be enclosed by
it, Ívarr took enough territory to found London. Infuriated, Ella
attacked, was captured and the 'blood-eagle' (see page 166) was carved
on his back. He died in agony. Ívarr decided to rule over England
from now on, and left the kingdom of Denmark to his brothers.

The Blood-Eagle

The blood-eagle rite is a legendary punishment, visited on particular enemies. The killers cut the ribs away from the spine, and then drag out the victim's lungs and arrange them across the back so that they look like wings, as a sacrifice to Óðinn. It's extremely unlikely that this punishment was ever carried out; the belief seems to originate from the misunderstanding of a verse in which an eagle, as a beast of battle, scores the dead Ella's back with his talons when feasting on the body. The mighty earl of Orkney, Torf-Einarr, is said to have killed a son of King Haraldr Fair-hair in this way, but these are the only two references in Old Norse tradition.

Rather like Sigurðr, Ragnarr never surpassed his first major adventure: killing the great serpent encircling Þóra's chamber. His duplicity in his dealings with his charismatic wife – killing her dog, ignoring her advice about consummating the marriage, and finally planning to marry the Swedish king's daughter – make him a rather unattractive hero. Ragnarr's sons, by contrast, listen to their mother's wisdom and conquer great swathes of territory. In Ívarr we have a new kind of hero, one who is seriously disabled, yet capable of leading an army. He is a master-strategist who uses brains rather than muscles.

⚔ THE MEN OF HRAFNISTA ⚔

One remarkable heroic lineage is that of Ketill hængr, whose nickname means 'salmon'. Ketill lived with his parents on the island of Hrafnista (modern Ramsta) in Norway and he was a troublesome lad, another 'coal-biter'. Ketill was no use around the house and argued a lot with his father, Hallbjörn Half-troll, but eventually he came good. Wandering in the northern part of the island one day

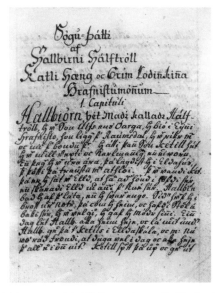

A late manuscript of *Ketils saga hœngs* (Ketill's Saga).

he encountered a flying dragon, fire spurting from its mouth and eyes. Ketill was used to going fishing in this part of the island, and he thought to himself that he'd never seen a fish quite like this one before. When the dragon attacked him, Ketill boldly cut it in half with his axe, and then told his father that he'd killed a rather large salmon – hence his nickname.

Ketill also finished off some cannibal giants who were attacking the folk of Hrafnista and had further adventures in the far north. A winter spent with a giant, Brúni, and his family resulted in a love-affair with Hrafnhildr, Brúni's daughter – and a son, Grímr Shaggy-cheek. Hallbjörn refused to accept Hrafnhildr as a daughter-in-law, however, calling her a troll (a bit rude from a man whose nickname was 'Half-troll') and Hrafnhildr sailed away from Hrafnista, leaving her child behind. Ketill gained some magic arrows and a splendid sword from a Lappish magician, Brúni's brother.

CHAPTER 5

Battle between a warrior and a female sea-troll. From the fourteenth-century Icelandic manuscript *Flateyjarbók*.

He became famous for troll-slaying and for battling against rogue Vikings, but he never forgot his troll-beloved, and when he married a human wife, he named his daughter Hrafnhildr in her memory.

Grímr took over Hrafnista when his father died. He was set to marry the daughter of a powerful lord when, seven nights before the wedding, she vanished. Evidence pointed to the involvement of the girl's stepmother, a woman originating from the far north, and suspected of having magical powers. Grímr journeyed there, and overcame several trollwomen and giants. Severely injured, he reluctantly accepted help from an extremely ugly trollwoman; her price for healing him was that he should kiss her, and finally, that they should share a bed. Grímr reluctantly consented, but he awakened in the morning to find that the hideous trollwoman, now freed from enchantment, was none other than his beloved Lofthæna, his missing fiancée. The reunited couple married and had a son: Arrow-Oddr.

Oddr inherited his grandfather's magic arrows, and had a long and eventful life. In his youth, a wandering seeress prophesied that, however far he might roam in his 300-year-long lifespan, his death would be caused by the head of his horse, Faxi. Oddr and his foster-brother rode the horse to a deserted valley, dug a deep pit and buried the creature alive. Thereafter Oddr had any number of adventures, fighting Vikings, gaining a magic shirt of invulnerability from an Irish princess, converting to Christianity and winning the great battle of Sámsey against the twelve berserk brothers, led by Angantýr (see below). Finally Oddr decided to revisit the haunts of his youth and came to the mound where the horse was buried. On top of it lay a horse's head, still covered with skin. Oddr, sure that he had long outlived the seeress's prophecy, prodded the head with his spear, tipping it over. Out from beneath it crawled an adder; it struck at Oddr, fastening its fangs in his foot. Oddr's leg swelled and turned black all the way up to his thigh, so he knew that his days were done. His men carried him down to the shore where he recited a long poem recounting his many glorious deeds. Then he died and his men burned his body on his ship. The line of the Hrafnista-men did not end there, however, for Hrafnhildr, Ketill's daughter, was the foremother of many famous men, including some of the Icelandic settlers who would later tell their ancestors' stories.

ᛟ TWELVE BERSERK BROTHERS ON AN ISLAND ᛟ

Oddr's greatest feat perhaps was the mighty battle he undertook, along with his great friend Hjálmarr, on the island of Sámsey (Samsø, between Sweden and Denmark). Angantýr and his eleven brothers were the sons of a great chieftain, and the second son, Hjörvarðr, was so proud of his reputation for raiding and harrying that he decided he would wed the daughter of the King of Sweden. The brothers all accompanied him to Uppsala on his wooing journey, and Hjörvarðr requested the princess's hand. But Hjálmarr the wise, who had long served the Swedish king, spoke up and asked

Berserker warriors from the Lewis Chessmen set, gnashing their shields.

Berserkir

Berserkir (berserkers) were a particular kind of warrior who would howl and bite their shields before battle. They may have worn bear-skins (hence their name, 'bear-shirts' – another term for them is *úlfheðnar* or 'wolf-pelts'), but the word *berserkir* may equally mean 'bare-shirts', fighters who wore no armour. In battle they became frenzied, lashing out without regard for their own safety. It's been suggested that they may have ingested some kind of hallucinogen to stimulate the battle-madness. In the sagas berserkers form anti-social gangs, going from household to household, threatening to rape the women unless someone is prepared to meet their leader in single combat. In one saga, the hero disposes of a berserk, who is gnashing his shield prior to fighting, by heaving the shield smartly upwards and thus tearing off his enemy's jaw!

if *he* might marry the lovely princess Ingibjörg. The king asked Ingibjörg to choose which suitor she preferred, and she declared for Hjálmarr, a man of good reputation, against the piratical Hjörvarðr and his *berserkir* brothers. Hjörvarðr promptly challenged Hjálmarr to a battle; the victor would marry Ingibjörg.

The brothers made their way to Sámsey where Hjálmarr and his friend Arrow-Oddr were waiting for them. Angantýr had had a foreboding dream about the battle, but his father had bolstered his courage by giving him a magic sword, Tyrfingr, forged by dwarfs, and guaranteed to bring victory. Hjálmarr was gloomy about his chances when he saw the brothers land on the island and prophesied that they would all be guests of Óðinn in Valhöll come the evening. Oddr rallied his friend and battle was joined.

The berserk-fit came over the brothers; they howled and gnashed at their shields. Hjálmarr decided to take on Angantýr and his magic sword, which shone like a sun-beam, while Oddr, wearing the enchanted shirt that the Irish princess had woven for him, fought against the rest.

Oddr slew all eleven brothers, but when he rejoined Hjálmarr, he found that although his friend had indeed killed Angantýr, he'd sustained sixteen wounds and was dying. Hjálmarr lamented his destiny, regretting that he, who owned five whole estates at home in Sweden, now lay dying on Sámsey. Never again would he hear the beautiful singing of the women of Uppsala, nor hold Ingibjörg in his arms. He gave Oddr a ring to take to the princess, asking him to tell her how heroically he had fallen. In his last verse, Hjálmarr faced up to his fate:

> *A raven flies from the high tree;*
> *the eagle flies along in company;*
> *I gave the eagle his last meal,*
> *he'll now be tasting my blood.*
> HJÁLMARR'S DEATH-SONG, V. 10

So Hjálmarr died; Oddr bore the news – and Hjálmarr's corpse – home to Sweden, where Ingibjörg too died of grief. Angantýr and his brothers were all entombed in burial mounds on Sámsey – along with the valuable sword, Tyrfingr.

☒ HERVÖR RECOVERS THE SWORD ☒

Angantýr had left behind a daughter, born posthumously, called Hervör. She grew up a bold and brave girl, refusing to sew or weave, for she preferred sword-play and spear-throwing. Her grandfather had tried to discipline her, but whenever she was rebuked she would run off into the forest and waylay men to steal their money. After some thralls insulted her, claiming that her father was a low-born man, Hervör learned the truth of her father's identity from her mother. She abandoned female clothing, joined a Viking crew and sailed for Sámsey.

Despite warnings that the island is an uncanny place, Hervör lands alone on the island and makes her way to the burial mounds. Here she invokes her father and uncles by name, demanding that Angantýr hand over the famous sword. The burial mounds, with eerie flames burning before them, yawn open and the dead men stand at their doors. Angantýr at first denies that he has the sword, then warns that a curse lies upon it – Hervör's descendants will slay one another with it – but at last he grudgingly hands it over, observing:

> *Young girl, I declare you're not like most men,*
> *hanging around mounds by night,*
> *with an engraved spear and in metal of the Goths [armour],*
> *a helmet and corslet before the hall-doors.*
> WAKING OF ANGANTÝR, V. 21

And truly Hervör is not like most men, nor most women either. Seizing the sword from the dead man's hands, she returns triumphantly to her ship where, for a good while, she continues her career as a Viking, raiding widely around the Baltic Sea. Hervör does eventually marry and has two sons, one named Angantýr, after her father, and the other Heiðrekr. Heiðrekr kills his brother in a sort of accident and is exiled; his mother gives him Tyrfingr as a gift.

Heiðrekr is shrewd and quick to outwit his enemies, though he does as much evil as good. He marries the daughter of the Emperor of Constantinople, and has a daughter, also called Hervör. King Heiðrekr has an enemy, a wise man called Gestumblindi, and the king summons him to court. Gestumblindi fears that the king means him harm, and so he is very relieved when a mysterious man arrives at his home and offers to go to the king in his place. The false Gestumblindi engages in a riddle-contest with Heiðrekr and finally confounds the king by asking the killer question, 'What did Óðinn whisper into Baldr's ear as he lay on the funeral pyre?' Heiðrekr, realizing that his opponent can be none other than the god himself, draws Tyrfingr and lunges at him. But Óðinn turns himself into a falcon, just finding

---

Gestumblindi's Riddles

The riddles of the fake Gestumblindi are rather mixed. Some are traditional: 'What did I drink yesterday that was neither water nor wine nor ale nor any kind of food?' (Answer: the morning dew.) Another is: 'What is that creature that has eight legs and four eyes and has its knees above its belly?' (Answer – of course – a spider.) Some are very obscure; the answer to one is: 'a dead horse on an ice-floe drifting down a river, with a serpent on the corpse' – not an easy one to guess. Tolkien got his inspiration for Bilbo's riddle-contest with Gollum in *The Hobbit* from this saga, though Bilbo's unanswerable question: 'What have I got in my pocket?' is rather different from the cosmic question about Baldr with which Óðinn concludes the contest.

---

time to curse Heiðrekr with meeting death at the hands of 'the worst of thralls'. Tyrfingr slices the falcon's tail-feathers (which is why falcons are short-tailed), but the god makes good his escape. And sure enough, soon afterwards, Heiðrekr is slain without honour in his bed by a cabal of well-born thralls whom he had captured and enslaved during his expeditions in the British Isles. The rest of the saga relates the continuing role of Tyrfingr in the fate of the dynasty and incorporates the famous battle of the Goths and Huns, in which Heiðrekr's two sons find themselves fighting on opposing sides. One does indeed slay the other with the accursed sword.

⚔ ETERNAL CONFLICT IN ORKNEY ⚔

In Chapter 2 we learned that Freyja brought about the Hjaðningavíg, the endless battle that will rage until *ragnarök*. This is how that battle came to be. Heðinn, the prince of Sarkland, met a woman in a forest clearing one day. She called herself Göndul (a well-known valkyrie name). Göndul encouraged Heðinn to visit King Högni and try his skills against him, to see who was the stronger. Högni was happy to take part in the contest, involving swimming, shooting, fighting and riding, and the two men turned out to be so evenly matched that they swore oaths of brotherhood to one another. Heðinn was still young; Högni was somewhat older and had a daughter called Hildr. Göndul appeared to Heðinn again, conceding that the two men were equals, except that Högni had a splendid queen, and Heðinn had none. To Heðinn's reply that he could marry Hildr if he asked for her, Göndul argued that he would do better to abduct Hildr and murder her mother. Then Högni would have no queen at all, while Heðinn would have proved his mettle in taking Hildr by force. Forgetting the oaths he had sworn, Heðinn acted on this plan. Högni returned home to find his wife dead and his daughter kidnapped, and he set out in pursuit, tracking Heðinn to the island

Scene perhaps representing the Hjaðningavíg. A sea-borne attack force meets a land-army, while a female figure stands between them. Lärbro Stora Hammars I picture-stone, Gotland.

of Hoy in Orkney. No mediation was possible, given the extent of Heðinn's crime, and so the two sides fell to fighting. Every night Hildr revived the slain, and every day battle was joined again, and so it will continue until *ragnarök*.

Göndul the supernatural troublemaker is likely a form of Freyja; we are told that she owns half the dead in one poem, and in the late version of the story she was forced to begin the conflict in order to recover the *Brisinga men* neck-ring from Óðinn. In other versions, Hildr is herself a valkyrie, and there's no need for Göndul to egg Heðinn on to his treachery. In what's probably the oldest version, Hildr was ready to mediate between her father and her lover, but Högni had one of those troublesome swords (probably also dwarf-forged, judging by its name, *Dáinsleif*, 'Dáinn's heirloom') which must always kill once unsheathed: thus battle could not be averted. Hildr loved both men so much that she could not bear for one to kill the other, hence her constantly restoring them to life to resume their eternal conflict.

Unlike the Völsungs, with their obsession with treasure and vengeance, these heroes pursue glory through travel and conquest of territory, through loyal service to a lord, and, quite often, by being smart and strategic. And clearly, as her father observes, the Viking girl Hervör is not like most other women, or men either, in her courage in claiming her patrimony from the dead. Nevertheless, all the heroes whose tales have been recounted in the last two chapters could be confident in finding their way to Valhöll after death, to join the *Einherjar*, the heroic dead who will fight on the side of the gods at *ragnarök*. Indeed the Hjaðningavíg seems set up for just such recruitment purposes, though it's confounded by Hildr's capacity to regenerate the fallen. In the final chapter we will see how *ragnarök* comes about – and learn what follows it.

6

~~~~~

END TIMES —
AND RENEWAL

As we know, Óðinn sacrificed his eye in Mímir's Well in order to gain knowledge of the future. Yet he still, obsessively, seeks out those who might be able to tell him more. *The Seeress's Prophecy* recounts a seeress's response to being questioned by Óðinn about past and future. Much of what follows in this chapter is drawn from her account. But Óðinn also visits the giant Vafþrúðnir; despite Frigg's warning him against the adventure, Óðinn sets out boldly and enters the giant's hall:

> *Greetings, Vafþrúðnir! Now I have come into the hall*
> *to see you in person;*
> *this I want to know first, whether you are wise*
> *or very wise, giant!*
> VAFÞRÚÐNIR'S SAYINGS, V. 6

Vafþrúðnir rises to the challenge, recognizing the invitation to participate in a wisdom contest, and he sets the stakes: 'we shall wager our heads in the hall, / guest, on our wisdom' (v. 19). God and giant exchange arcane lore, about the distant past, the history of the gods, and about the future: the events of *ragnarök*. Wisdom contests are complex undertakings, for the idea is as much to catch out the opponent as to learn from him or her, and both contenders must know enough to discern whether the other party is lying. At the end of this contest, Óðinn seems to have heard enough about *ragnarök* and what comes after it, and he concludes with his favourite unanswerable question:

> *Much have I travelled, much have I tried out,*
> *much have I tested the Powers;*
> *what did Óðinn say into his son's ear*
> *before he mounted the pyre?*
> VAFÞRÚÐNIR'S SAYINGS, V. 54

And with this question Vafþrúðnir knows that the game is up, for only Óðinn can know the answer. The poem ends with this admission; we assume that Vafþrúðnir must surrender his head, though whether Óðinn takes it may be another matter.

Why does Óðinn embark on this quest for wisdom, risking his own neck to verify the information that he has? One likely reason is a compulsive need to check – and double-check – whether fate is really ineluctable. Is there any possibility that one of the universe's many wise beings knows of a different narrative about the future? Must Óðinn meet the wolf and be devoured by him? Must the world plunge headlong, engulfed in flames, before vanishing under the sea? As we know, and as the god repeatedly hears from those he questions, *ragnarök* will indeed come one day. The signs of the world's destruction are already beginning to manifest themselves, for Óðinn's clever question shows that one of the portents of the end has already occurred; Baldr, best and brightest of the gods, is dead.

⚔ THE DEATH OF BALDR ⚔

We have not heard much about Baldr so far, and that's primarily because little more is narrated about him than the events surrounding his death. Snorri assures us that he is radiantly handsome (so much so that a flower, *baldrsbrá*, a kind of camomile, is named after his eyelashes). Clever, wise, kindly, married to Nanna, Baldr is loved by everyone.

One day, however, he begins to have ominous dreams and, after their usual consultation, the gods resolve to ask every created thing to swear an oath not to harm him. In one poem, *Baldrs Draumar* (Baldr's Dreams), Óðinn himself, like any anxious father, saddles up his mount Sleipnir and sets out for Hel's kingdom to find out the truth of the matter. But on the edge of Hel's kingdom, he meets a blood-stained pup (a young hell-hound perhaps) and instead of

Óðinn rides Sleipnir to visit Hel, past a bloody-chested pup.
W. G. Collingwood (1908).

pressing forward to Hel's hall, he decides to awaken a dead seeress whose grave lies nearby. As in his other dialogues with the wise, Óðinn dissembles his identity. The grumpy seeress confirms her questioner's fears:

For whom are the benches decked with arm-rings,
is the dais so fairly strewn with gold? [...]

Here mead stands, brewed for Baldr,
clear liquor; a shield hangs above,
the Æsir are in dread anticipation.
Reluctantly I told you, now I'll be silent.
BALDR'S DREAMS, VV. 6–7

The seeress imparts further details to Óðinn until he brings the conversation to an end by posing another mysterious question – apparently a riddle about waves. This is enough to reveal his identity and the seeress refuses to converse further.

Baldr seems then to be doomed. In Snorri's account it's Frigg, the god's energetic mother, who works her way through creation, taking the oaths of everything to refuse to harm her son. 'Fire and water, iron and all kinds of metal, stones, the earth, wood, sickness, animals, birds, poison, serpents' – all swear to do him no harm. What then could bring about the god's death? Frigg had not bothered with the lowly mistletoe, for it seemed to her too young and tender, and she lets slip this information to an inquisitive woman who visits her in her hall, Fensalir. That was her mistake, for the woman was Loki in disguise, and he makes good use of this information.

Meanwhile, the gods are amusing themselves mightily at their meeting-place. Baldr stands in the middle and the others hurl missiles at him. All their weapons bounce harmlessly off him – a temptation to complacency, perhaps. Standing sadly at the edge of the group is Höðr, Baldr's brother, who is blind, and who can't take part in the game. But here is a friendly voice in his ear, asking if he wants a go; a slender dart is slipped into his hand and the speaker guides his aim so that it hits its mark (see page 40). Baldr falls; a great wail goes up from all the gods and Loki slips away in the hubbub. The mistletoe dart has brought down the best of the gods. Óðinn is doubly grief-stricken; not only is his son dead, but he knows that this death is a clear portent of *ragnarök*.

Frigg promises all her favour to anyone who will ride to Hel to negotiate Baldr's return, and a man called Hermóðr leaps on Sleipnir and sets off. Baldr's funeral is prepared; his body is taken to the shore and placed on his ship. But the ship will not slide down the rollers into the sea until a giantess called Hyrrokin appears, riding a wolf with serpents for reins. Hyrrokin launches the ship with a single push, so mighty that sparks fly and all the lands quake; despite this service she narrowly escapes being obliterated by Þórr. Nanna dies of grief at this and her body is laid beside Baldr's on the pyre. Flames engulf the two bodies, witnessed by all kinds of beings who have gathered to do Baldr honour. An unfortunate dwarf, Litr, gets under

The death of Baldr. Christoffer William Eckersberg (1817).

Viking Ship-Burials

High-born men and women were often buried in ships in the Viking Age, symbolizing perhaps the journey the dead had to make to the Other World. The Oseberg ship, described in the Introduction, is only one such archaeological find. In Britain, the seventh-century Anglo-Saxon king buried at Sutton Hoo was also interred on a ship (though nothing has survived of it but its rivets), proving that this was not exclusively a Viking-Age custom. In the ninth century, an Arab traveller, Ibn Fadlan, encountered some Viking Rus warriors on the Volga. Their chieftain had just died and Ibn Fadlan gives a detailed account of the funeral rites. There is no space to describe them in full here, but at the culmination of the ceremony the chieftain's ship, on which his corpse is lying, is set ablaze with a flaming torch, borne by the dead man's next of kin. He circles the ship stark naked and walking backwards, covering his anus with one hand. And, says Ibn Fadlan, so much wood was piled round the ship and such a brisk wind sprang up that within an hour, ship, chieftain and all were consumed to ashes.

A Viking funeral-ship is set ablaze and pushed out to sea.
Frank Dicksee (1893).

Þórr's feet as he steps forward to consecrate the pyre and is straight away kicked into it.

Hermóðr bravely made his way down to Hel, and found its ruler not entirely unsympathetic to the gods' request. Baldr and Nanna were already present in the hall, Baldr sitting in the high seat no less. Hel stipulated that Baldr might return to the world of the living if all things were to weep for him, and Hermóðr headed back with the news. The Æsir quickly mobilized on hearing Hel's conditions and messengers were sent out all over the world. They met with great success, persuading everything to weep for Baldr – even metals (the origin of condensation, Snorri tells us). But in a cave they found a

---

The Rape of Rindr

Óðinn knows that Baldr's avenger must be born of Rindr, a human princess. Impregnating her is not altogether a straightforward task. Rindr resists the ugly old god's advances; though he insinuates himself into her father's household, where he operates as a very successful general, his first attempt at a kiss gets him only a slap across the face. Next, he becomes a metal-worker and brings Rindr beautifully made bracelets; this is no more effective and another slap follows. Finally he bewitches her, using runes to send her mad. Then, disguising himself as an old woman, Óðinn pretends to be a healer. He prescribes a horribly bitter drink, one so vile that Rindr must be tied to the bed so that she can't refuse to swallow it. And, left alone with the patient, the apparent healer rapes the unhappy girl. The other gods, so this story (related by Saxo Grammaticus) tells us, were so horrified by this behaviour that Óðinn was sent into exile. Rindr, however, became pregnant and gave birth to Váli.

---

giantess called, ironically, Þökk (Thanks). When asked to weep for Baldr she retorted:

> *Þökk will weep*
> *dry tears*
> *for Baldr's funeral.*
> *Living nor dead*
> *I get no joy of any man's son:*
> *let Hel hold what she has.*
> THE TRICKING OF GYLFI, CH. 49

And it is strongly suspected that this uncooperative giantess was none other than Loki.

The aftermath of Baldr's death was twofold. Óðinn had learned from the dead seeress that only one man could avenge Baldr, and that he was not yet born.

Little Váli was indeed prodigious; like Helgi, he was ready to fight at one night old, says *The Seeress's Prophecy*:

He never washed his hands
nor combed his hair
until he brought Baldr's adversary
to the funeral pyre.
THE SEERESS'S PROPHECY, V. 33

But it is the poor blind brother, Höðr, 'the slayer by hand' – not Loki, 'the slayer by plan', the one behind the murder – whom Váli kills. For Loki's fate is written differently.

Why must Baldr die? He's often been compared with other gods who perish through some horrible accident or conspiracy. Ancient Near Eastern figures such as the Egyptian Osiris, or Attis, the beloved of Cybele, also die; the context of their myths suggests that this occurs in a seasonal cycle and resurrection comes with the spring. Isis succeeds in reconstituting Osiris, her brother/lover, as the Nile rises again every year to fertilize the land, and Attis too is reborn annually. But Baldr's resurrection (at least for now) fails. A fertility dimension to the myth seems unlikely, therefore.

Baldr may be a sacrifice; certainly being pierced by a missile is congruent with sacrifice to Óðinn. Yet no benefit seems to accrue from Baldr's death; if he is a sacrifice, it seems a pointless one (unlike Óðinn's own sacrifice of himself to gain the secret of the runes). The myth speaks to the horror of conflict within kin-groups; vengeance cannot be achieved by killing the perpetrator, for Váli's vengeance on Höðr simply eliminates yet another of Óðinn's sons. Who should take vengeance for Höðr? In this respect, Óðinn is fortunate in that he can sire new sons, replacing those who die. But, as the myth acknowledges, sons are not *so* interchangeable; Váli cannot truly take Baldr's place.

⚔ THE BINDING OF LOKI ⚔

Snorri follows his account of the failure to weep Baldr out of Hel with the gods' swift pursuit, capture and binding of Loki. In the poetic tradition, Loki's binding is consequent on his final rupture with his fellow-gods. Remember the feast at Ægir's hall – the one that required Hymir's extra-enormous cauldron? All the gods and goddesses were there, except for Þórr who was away as usual smiting giants in the east, and Loki, who was *persona non grata*. Yet he presents himself coolly at the hall and demands to be assigned a seat and given a drink. Bragi, the god of poetry, is ready to refuse him, but, once Loki invokes the blood-brother relationship between himself and Óðinn, and reminds the god that he had sworn never to drink unless Loki were offered drink too, Óðinn decrees that the 'Father of the Wolf' must be admitted.

In the poem *Loki's Quarrel* which relates this tale, Loki now proceeds systematically to insult each of the gods in turn. The pattern is quite uniform; Loki insults god A, god A replies, Loki responds, and god B speaks up in A's defence, only to draw Loki's bad-mouthing down upon himself. The gods are subjected to a range of calumnies: Óðinn has performed *seiðr* (see Chapter 2) and is an oath-breaker; other gods are cowards or have been disgraced in some way. Njörðr is accused of letting Hymir's daughters (giantesses, here probably symbolizing rivers) piss in his mouth, as the rivers run into the sea, and of having fathered his children on his sister. The goddesses are charged with sexual promiscuity, often with having had sex with Loki himself, or, like Skaði, they are reminded of Loki's role in their kinsman's death. Frigg is taunted with the loss of Baldr, and Freyja with having slept with every man within the hall – including her own brother. Even Sif, Þórr's wife, is charged with having slept with Loki, and we wonder just *how* it was that Loki was able to steal Sif's wonderful golden hair. Finally Þórr arrives and with his habitual bellowing and threats puts a stop to Loki's barbs – notwithstanding

A strangely horned Loki, bound after his capture by Þórr,
on the eighth-century Kirkby Stephen stone, Cumbria.

some telling remarks about Þórr's behaviour in the Skrýmir adventure (see Chapter 3). And then Loki leaves:

but for you alone I shall go out
for I know that you do strike.
LOKI'S QUARREL, V. 64, LL. 4–6

That may be a crack about the master-builder and the oath-breaking that inaugurated Ásgarðr's new walls; maybe it's a rueful recognition of the risks involved in annoying Þórr. As far as we can tell from other sources, most of what Loki says is true, though he puts a disreputable gloss on Týr's sacrifice of his hand, and Freyr's willingness to give Skírnir his sword in order to win Gerðr. *Loki's Quarrel* is a very funny poem, but its humour is charged with horror, both at Loki's shamelessness and at the revelations about the gods. Is the poem a serious critique of the pagan deities – perhaps composed by a Christian who wants to reveal them as hypocrites and cowards? Or is the poem the work of someone who was secure in his belief, who wanted to show that the gods are indeed different from us – and that their fulfilment of their divine functions cannot be comprehended within human ethical frameworks? Very likely *Loki's Quarrel* was understood differently at different times in its existence; much depends on the nuance imparted by the performer. But it's not hard to feel by the end of it that perhaps the world will be better off without this rabble.

Loki made good his escape from the furious gods, turning himself into a salmon and hiding in a waterfall. Snorri's account of his capture elaborates on this. Loki built himself a house in the mountains near the waterfall and lurked underwater by day. One evening he began to speculate about how the Æsir might manage to catch him in his fish-form. Picking up some linen thread, he made a prototype fishing-net. Then, realizing that Óðinn had spotted him from his high seat Hliðskjálf, and that the gods were on their way to the hideout, he quickly threw the net in the fire and dived into the water. The wisest of the gods (named here as Kvasir, the one whose blood gave rise to the mead of poetry) saw the pattern the net made in the ashes and deduced what its purpose must be. The gods quickly replicated the device and, although salmon-Loki jumped over it, he was eventually captured in mid-leap by Þórr who had waded into the middle of the river. Though Loki slithered as fast as he could through Þórr's hands, his tail caught in the god's fist; this explains why salmon taper markedly towards the tail and why they leap out of the water when making their way upstream.

Loki now finds himself in peril; he has not surrendered to the gods under pre-arranged conditions, but rather he is their captive. The gods take three great flat rocks, set them edge upwards and make a hole in each slab. Loki's sons are seized and transformed into wolves; Nari tears his brother Narfi into pieces, and the gods use Narfi's guts to bind his father to the rock. The guts tighten

Loki's wife Sigyn holds the bowl to catch the poison dripping from the serpent that Skaði has hung over him. Mårten Eskil Winge (1890).

magically into iron bonds; as a final flourish, Skaði hangs a poison-ous serpent over Loki's face, venom dripping from its fangs. And Sigyn, Loki's wife, now stands by her husband holding a basin to catch the poison. Every now and then she must turn away to empty it, and when the venom falls onto Loki's face, he writhes horribly in his bonds – the cause of earthquakes.

Loki's final break with the Æsir raises some interesting ques-tions. His usual mode of operation has been as an ambivalent figure, siding inconsistently with the giants, but also helping the gods recover stolen items, and he has a particular role as Þórr's sidekick. Why this, now? One suggestion links Loki's behaviour to the various prophecies concerning *ragnarök*. Just as Fenrir must first be bound if he is to break his fetters and attack the gods on that final day, so Loki must also be confined if he is to sunder his bonds to lead the giants against his former companions. And thus he must provoke the gods into binding him, through the twin offences of bringing about Baldr's death and by his bravura display of insults in *Loki's Quarrel*. If Baldr's death is a portent of *ragnarök*, then Baldr must die, and Loki must be bound. This assumes a chronological coherence to the tales surviving from what must have been a great corpus of varying myths originating in different parts of the Norse-speaking world. But even if the idea of Loki possessing a master-plan strains credulity, there's certainly a strong sense that the fate of the gods is already determined, that, despite Óðinn's efforts to see whether the prophesied future can be falsified or forestalled, the end is already written. Suggestive too, as noted above, is the fact that Snorri knows one of Loki's sons (the brother-killing wolf) as Váli, sharing the name of Óðinn's newly begotten son who kills his half-brother Höðr in vengeance for his other half-brother Baldr. Themes of fratricide, of vengeance, of those apocalyptic beasts, wolves and serpents, run through these two tales in a way that underlines the fundamental link between the two gods, Óðinn and Loki.

⚔ SIGNS OF THE LAST TIMES ⚔

First comes the Great Winter, the *fimbulvetr*. Three winters run into one another, with no intervening summers; snow drives from all directions with biting winds and sharp frost. Social dislocation follows:

> *Brother will fight brother and be his slayer,*
> *sisters' sons will violate the kinship-bond;*
> *hard it is in the world, whoredom abounds,*
> *axe-age, sword-age, shields are cleft asunder,*
> *wind-age, wolf-age, before the world plunges headlong;*
> *no man will spare another.*
> THE SEERESS'S PROPHECY, V. 45

Punishing Sinners – A Christian Concept?
Near a place called Corpse-strand, the seeress sees a cloudy and
turbulent river where those who swear false oaths, murderers and
seducers of other men's wives are wading. Another river flows down
from the east, called Fearful; it's filled with axes and knives. That there
are Other World punishments for human sinners is not an idea found
elsewhere in Norse myth; the inclusion of these torments suggests
Christian influence. Given that the version of the poem in the Codex
Regius may have been composed around the time that Norway was
converting to Christianity (1000 CE), this is not impossible.

The world drives forward into chaos. Before mankind falls into
civil war, the seeress summons up other indications of the end times.

Deep in Gallows-wood a cock with sooty-red plumage crows.
Another is heard in Ironwood where a trollwoman is nurturing
Fenrir's offspring: the wolves who pursue the sun and the moon.
The uncannily discordant soundscape of the end is punctuated by
the howling of the great hound Garmr (maybe a double of Fenrir, or
a quite independent monstrous beast, a kind of hell or Hel-hound).
Now comes the terrible moment when both the heavenly bodies are
engulfed by the gaping jaws of the beasts who have so long pursued
them and the world is plunged into darkness.

Now Yggdrasill catches fire. The great ash tree totters, and
Heimdallr sounds the alarm by blowing his mighty Gjallar-horn.
Óðinn takes emergency counsel with Mímir's head, but it is too late
to hope for advice from that quarter now. The mountains quake,
driving the dwarfs outside where they stand groaning before their
rocky doors. Trollwomen wander the roads; humans don't know
what to do. The *Einherjar* ride out to face the battle for which they've
been training all these millennia, but – or so Fáfnir the dragon
prophesied to Sigurðr in his dying moments – as they and the gods
journey from Óskópnir (Not-yet-made), the island where the final

The Great Wolf

There's a terrifying description of the great wolf Managarm (Garmr or Hound of the Moon) in Alan Garner's 1960 novel, *The Weirdstone of Brisingamen*. Garner makes use of quite a lot of Old Norse myth in the novel; at its culmination, a dark and terrible magic is unleashed:

> Racing out of the north was a cloud, lower than any that hid the sun and black. Monstrous it was, and in shape a ravening wolf. Its loins fell below the horizon, and its lean body arched across the sky to pounding shoulders, and a head with jaws agape that even now was over the far end of the valley ... All the sky to the north and east was wolf head. The mouth yawned wider, till there was nothing to be seen but the black, cavernous maw, rushing down to swallow hill and valley whole.
>
> Alan Garner, *The Weirdstone of Brisingamen*, London 2010, p. 283

Luckily the magic of the Weirdstone dispels the horror, and the world is saved.

---

battle takes place, the rainbow bridge Bifröst breaks and their horses founder in the river. Victory is snatched away from them.

The forces of terror are unleashed from each of the cardinal points. From the south comes the fire-giant Surtr, bearing an

The gods prepare for *ragnarök*. Drawn by W. G. Collingwood (1908) in the style of a Viking-Age sculpture.

enormous sword from which the sun glances in dazzling brilliance. The sinister corpse-ship Naglfari, made of dead men's nails, has set sail from the east with fire-giants as its crew; Loki is its steersman, bringing fiery destruction to the worlds of gods and men. Also advancing from the east comes Hrymr, another frost-giant leader, and in the ocean the huge coils of the Miðgarðs-serpent are thrashing. And Fenrir, finally, has snapped the silken fetter that has held him in thrall all these ages and is loping on the loose.

✗ THE LAST BATTLE AND THE DEATHS OF THE GODS ✗

Now the long-prophesied single combats come to pass. Óðinn walks boldly forward to face the wolf, but the god of the spear finds that Gungnir is of no help to him, and Fenrir swallows him in one mighty gulp. Frigg weeps to see her husband die; 'Frigg's dear-beloved', the poem calls him, comparing his death to that of Baldr, as 'Frigg's second sorrow'. The goddesses mourn on the sidelines as the gods shoulder their shields against their mortal foes. Next up is Þórr, encountering once again his old enemy, the Miðgarðs-serpent. The god brings the great snake down but, staggering only nine paces away from the corpse, he too falls, overcome by the serpent's might and venomous breath.

Snorri adds some details which are not known from anywhere else; they may be traditional or may be the product of his own instinct for organization. Freyr goes against Surtr, and now, as Loki foretold, he must surely regret the lack of the sword he gave away for the giant-girl Gerðr. The great dog Garmr, whose terrible howling presaged *ragnarök*, brings down Týr; that god's past history with Fenrir gives rise to the suspicion that Garmr and Fenrir are indeed the same, and that the wolf has unfinished business with the god whose hand he snapped off. Heimdallr and Loki contend against one another – not for the first time – and each slaughters the other.

Sleipnir stumbles as Fenrir leaps on Óðinn. Dorothy Hardy (1909).

The gods do make some headway against the monsters. Víðarr, Óðinn's son, leaps into Fenrir's maw; his feet are protected from the wolf's fangs by the thick-soled shoes he wears. Every time sole-material is clipped from toes or heels, Snorri tells us in an aside, this contributes to Víðarr's footwear. With one hand he reaches to the wolf's upper jaw and tears him asunder. This image, the death of the father and the vengeance of the son, is a favourite of Viking-Age sculptors.

Heimdallr and Loki in Conflict

Tradition tells us that Heimdallr and Loki have met in combat before. On that occasion, they fought out in the sea on a skerry called Singasteinn, both adopting seal-form for the battle. The bone of contention was possession of the *Brisinga men*, Freyja's great neck-ring, which had somehow come into Loki's hands. Heimdallr wins the fight and restores the precious jewelry to the goddess; this is probably a version of the tale of Loki's theft that was related in Chapter 2.

Víðarr steps into Fenrir's maw on the early tenth-century
Gosforth Cross, Cumbria.

Now the giant Surtr's fire sets the whole world ablaze and the
process by which the earth was made at the beginning of *The Seeress's
Prophecy* (as recounted in Chapter 2) is thrown into reverse:

> *The sun turns black, land sinks into the sea;*
> *the bright stars vanish from the sky;*
> *steam rises up in the conflagration,*
> *hot flame plays high against heaven itself.*
> THE SEERESS'S PROPHECY, V. 57

A Volcanic Catastrophe?

Since *The Seeress's Prophecy* has been dated to around the year 1000,
well after the settlement of Iceland, it has been mooted that the
description of *ragnarök* that it contains reflects the island's volcanic
nature. Certainly in the verse cited above, features of a volcanic eruption
– flames shooting upwards, the darkness as the ash-cloud obscures
the sun, the disappearance of the land under the red-hot lava flows,
and the sizzle of the black molten rock meeting the sea – could all
be read into the poem's vision of the end of the world.

That the sun has already been swallowed up by the wolf that has pursued it for aeons shows how the poems and Snorri's prose tradition seek to integrate different traditions into coherent narratives. Darkness, relieved only by the leaping flames, brings the end of the world.

⚡ REBIRTH ⚡

The end of the world, as the sea surges over the land and fiery destruction rains down on an earth where gods, men and even giants have all perished, marks the end of Time in Christian tradition. Not so in other mythologies, however; many systems imagine time and space as cyclical, and believe that, once the old, corrupt world has been swept away, a new one arises to take its place. For, although in eddic poetry the phrase *ragnarök* means 'doom of the Powers', Snorri uses a slightly different word, *rökkr*, which means something like 'dusk' or 'glimmering' – hence Wagner's understanding of the end of his heroic world as 'The Twilight of the Gods'. *Rökkr* could equally mean 'half-light before dawn' as well as 'twilight', and thus *rökkr* can usher in a new, brilliant day.

And this indeed is what we find, in the poetic tradition and in Snorri's account, derived from it. For the seeress whose vision constitutes *The Seeress's Prophecy* looks beyond the end of the world, and:

She sees, coming up a second time,
earth from the ocean, eternally green;
the waterfalls plunge, an eagle soars above them,
over the mountain, hunting fish.

The Æsir find one another on Iðavellir,
and they converse about the mighty Earth-Girdler,
and Fimbultýr's ancient runes.

There will be found again in the grass
the wonderful golden chequers,
those which they possessed in the bygone days.
THE SEERESS'S PROPHECY, VV. 59–61

For some of the Æsir will return. Amazingly, Hœnir, that mysterious third who walked beside Óðinn in many important moments in the past, comes back. And so too, wonderfully, the unwitting slayer and the sacrificial victim, Höðr and Baldr, return from the other side of death (the secret that Óðinn whispers into his dead son's ear on the pyre, we surmise). A new golden age is signalled: fields yield their crops without sowing, all harms are healed, and the golden chequers, so resonantly symbolic of the earlier age of innocence, are found once more on the plain. With the dazed air of survivors of a great catastrophe, the new Æsir reminisce about the Miðgarðs-serpent and the runes which Óðinn won for them.

The giant Vafþrúðnir too, in his wisdom contest with Óðinn, back in the old world, had foreseen the renewal that follows the cataclysm, revealing to the anxious god that some humans, with the promising names of Líf and Lífþrasir (Life and perhaps Life-thruster,

After the earth is reborn, an eagle flies past a waterfall, hunting for fish.
Emil Doepler (1905).

male and female maybe) survive by hiding in Hoddmímir's wood (perhaps Yggdrasill, given that great ash's proximity to Mímir's Well). The sun too, before she was swallowed by Fenrir, gave birth to a daughter who will travel on her mother's paths. Vafþrúðnir identifies further Æsir who will form the new generation of gods: Víðarr, avenger of his father Óðinn; Váli, avenger of his brother Baldr; Móði and Magni, Þórr's two sons, who will wield Mjöllnir, their father's weapon. Vafþrúðnir's vision is less optimistic than the vision of the seeress; the return of the sons of Óðinn and Þórr suggests the resumption of the old patterns of living, of vengeance and violence reasserting themselves. There's none of the emphasis on reconciliation that we find in *The Seeress's Prophecy*, no mention of the twin victims of Loki's terrible malice, Höðr and Baldr, coming to terms, their brotherhood renewed.

Even in the new world envisioned by the seeress, and despite the miraculous return of the lost golden chequers, there are signs that ineluctable systems are again at work, that the clock is ticking down to the next renewal. Once Hœnir has set up home in Óðinn's former territory he begins to cut 'wooden slips for prophecy'; fate is still operating. The very last thing that the seeress sees before she sinks down in her trance is the dragon Níðhöggr, the monstrous serpent who used to attack Yggdrasill, flying through the sky bearing corpses in his wings. This seems ominous. Some have suggested that this detail marks the seeress's return to the 'now' of her vision, and that, as her prophecy draws to its close, she sees the flight of the dragon in the present. Others have wondered whether Níðhöggr has a positive role in the new world, and is clearing away the last vestiges of the final battle by carrying off the corpses. But there's no compelling reason to think that the new world will not go the same way as the old, that evil and corruption will not manifest themselves once again (perhaps through a different vector from Loki and his giant allies), and that *ragna rökkr*, the dark before the dawn, will fall again – and again – through the cycle of the ages.

The Jelling Stone, a tenth-century Danish picture-stone,
commissioned by King Harald Bluetooth. It depicts the
crucified Christ in traditional runestone style.

A New God?

A version of *The Seeress's Prophecy* that was written down in the early
fourteenth century contains an extra verse at the point where the new
generation of gods has moved into the golden-roofed hall of Gimlé,
when the world has begun anew.

> Then comes the mighty one to the judgment of the Powers,
> full of strength, from above, he who rules over all.

Who can this mighty one be who comes to the reconstituted council
of the gods? Is this Jesus, returned for the Last Judgment, ready to call
time on the pagan pantheon, and to announce that the new religion
is truly here to stay?

☒ MYTHS LIVING ON ☒

By the time that the 'mighty one' descended to take charge, in the early fourteenth century, Iceland had long been Christian. Yet the Old Norse myths and legends still had resonance. Some new poems were being composed around this time, incorporating mythological and legendary motifs into traditional forms, but telling fresh stories. In one fourteenth-century poem a hero is cursed by his wicked stepmother to woo the unattainable maiden Menglöð. Young Svipdagr first visits his dead mother's grave-mound to obtain some protective spells and advice and then journeys to Menglöð's castle. A hostile giant who guards it won't let him in and the two embark on a long discussion of what tasks he must fulfil to gain entry. But these are impossibly circular; to complete the first task, Svipdagr would already have had to have performed the last. The situation is hopeless, unless – as his interlocutor explains – his name should happen to be Svipdagr! And immediately the gates swing open, the hero enters and the lovely Menglöð is taking him in her arms, demanding to know what took him so long.

Some myths and legends were converted into ballads and remained in the popular imagination. Though it's unlikely that anyone believed in Óðinn and Þórr any longer, the gods and heroes remained useful to think with, their stories reminding people of the importance of poetry, of cleverness and courage, of standing up to evil and of laughing in the face of death. Icelandic did not change much as a language over the centuries, and the myths preserved in sagas and poems were still understood. In the seventeenth century, the Codex Regius poems were edited, and translated into Latin; soon knowledge of them was circulating widely through Europe. The first English translations appeared in the eighteenth century (some containing hilarious errors), and the myths and legends of the north were popularized by the Brothers Grimm and Richard Wagner in Germany, and by William Morris and J. R. R. Tolkien in Britain. Now, with such popular cultural phenomena as *Game of Thrones* (with its constant threat of the Fimbulvetr, the Mighty Winter), Viking Death Metal or the *Vikings* TV series, whose hero is the very Ragnarr Shaggy-breeches whom we met in Chapter 5, the Scandinavian myths and legends are as vibrant today as at any time since Christianity displaced them from the hearts and minds of the north.

The original sources for most of the myths discussed in this book are fairly easy to get hold of in translation.

Snorri Sturluson, *Edda*, trans. Anthony Faulkes, 2nd edition (London, 2008). This contains *The Tricking of Gylfi* (*Gylfaginning*) and other mythological stories.

The Poetic Edda, trans. Carolyne Larrington, 2nd edition (Oxford, 2014). Most of the poems quoted in this book can be found in full here.

Saxo Grammaticus, The History of the Danes, ed. Hilda Ellis Davidson, trans. Peter Fisher (Cambridge, 1979)

Other interesting and readable books about Norse myth include:

Chris Abram, *Myths of the Pagan North: Gods of the Norsemen* (London and New York, 2011)

R. I. Page, *Norse Myths* (The Legendary Past) (London, 1990)

Heather O'Donoghue, *From Asgard to Valhalla: The Remarkable History of the Norse Myths* (London, 2007)

A scholarly but extremely interesting discussion of the myths is:

Margaret Clunies Ross, *Prolonged Echoes* Vol. 1 (Odense, 1994)

For a very readable account of the history of the Viking Age:

Anders Winroth, *The Age of the Vikings* (Princeton, 2015)

A more academic work:

Judith Jesch, *The Viking Diaspora* (London and New York, 2015)

A fascinating account of Scandinavian archaeology and its relation to myth:

Anders Andrén, *Tracing Old Norse Cosmology: The World Tree, Middle Earth and the Sun in Archaeological Perspective* (Lund, 2014)

Another exploration of Viking-Age archaeology:

Neil Price, *The Viking Way: Religion and War in the Iron Age of Scandinavia*, 2nd edition (Oxford, 2016)

There are of course numerous retellings for children, by authors such as Roger Lancelyn Green and Barbara Leonie Picard. Best of the bunch is:

Kevin Crossley-Holland, *The Penguin Book of Norse Myths: Gods of the Vikings* (London, 1996)

A fascinating series of novels based on the Norse myths – the first two for young adults, the last for older readers:

Joanne Harris, *Runemarks* (London, 2008)
Joanne Harris, *Runelight* (London, 2011)
Joanne Harris, *The Gospel of Loki* (London, 2014)

Two young adult novels based on the heroic legends:

Melvin Burgess, *Bloodtide* (London, 1999)
Melvin Burgess, *Bloodsong* (London, 2005)

All translations are the author's own, except:

page 17: 'engraved the letters of their own language …' from Saxo Grammaticus, *The History of the Danes*, ed. Hilda Ellis Davidson, trans. Peter Fisher (Cambridge, 1979), page 5

page 18: 'a man ... widely believed throughout Europe, though falsely, to be a god' from Saxo Grammaticus, *The History of the Danes*, ed. Hilda Ellis Davidson, trans. Peter Fisher (Cambridge, 1979), page 25

page 158: 'womanish body movements' from Saxo Grammaticus, *The History of the Danes*, ed. Hilda Ellis Davidson, trans. Peter Fisher (Cambridge, 1979), page 172

Images are listed by page numbers:

1 British Museum, London **2** Manx Museum, Isle of Man/Werner Forman Archive **8–9** Map by Martin Lubikowski, ML Design, London **10** Artwork by Drazen Tomic **13** Photo Fred Jones **14**, **16** Árni Magnússon Institute for Icelandic Studies, Reykjavík **18** Photo Gernot Keller **20** Jamtli Historieland Östersund **22** from Olaus Magnus, *A Description of the Northern Peoples*, 1555 (Hakluyt Society) **23** Bjorn Grotting/Alamy **24** Gerda Henkel Foundation **25** Werner Forman Archive **26**, **27** (**left**) Nationalmuseet, Copenhagen **27** (**right**) Statens Historiska Museet, Stockholm **32** Árni Magnússon Institute for Icelandic Studies, Reykjavík **33** Interfoto/Alamy **34** from Olive Bray, *Sæmund's Edda*, 1908 (The Viking Club) **37** National Museum of Art, Stockholm **39** Árni Magnússon Institute for Icelandic Studies, Reykjavík **40** from Abbie Farwell Brown, *In the Days of the Giants: A Book of Norse Tales*, 1902 (Houghton, Mifflin and Co.) **42**, **43** Árni Magnússon Institute for Icelandic Studies, Reykjavík **44** from Martin Oldenbourg, *Walhall, die Götterwelt der Germanen*, 1905 (Berlin) **45** from Felix Dahn, *Walhall: Germanische Götter- und Heldensagen*, 1901 (Breitkopf und Härtel) **46** Private Collection **48** Árni Magnússon Institute for Icelandic Studies, Reykjavík **49** from Olive Bray, *Sæmund's Edda*, 1908 (The Viking Club) **50** Árni Magnússon Institute for Icelandic Studies, Reykjavík **52** Photo Blood of Ox **53** from Mary H. Foster, *Asgard Stories: Tales from Norse Mythology*, 1901 (Silver, Burdett and Company) **54** from Martin Oldenbourg, *Walhall, die Götterwelt der Germanen*, 1905 (Berlin) **58** from Karl Gjellerup, *Den ældre Eddas Gudesange*, 1895 (Copenhagen) **59** Árni Magnússon Institute for Icelandic Studies, Reykjavík **61** Nationalmuseet, Copenhagen **63** Johnston (Frances Benjamin) Collection/Library of Congress, Washington, D.C. **64** Det Kongelige Bibliotek, Copenhagen **65** Árni Magnússon Institute for Icelandic Studies, Reykjavík **67** from Karl Gjellerup, *Den ældre Eddas Gudesange*, 1895 (Copenhagen) **68** Photo Carolyne Larrington **69** Photo Jan Taylor **71** from Abbie Farwell Brown, *In the Days of Giants: A Book of Norse Tales*, 1902 (Houghton, Mifflin and Co.) **72** Moesgaard Museum, Højbjerg/Dagli Orti/The Art Archive **73** from A. & E. Keary, *The Heroes of Asgard: Tales from Scandinavian Mythology*, 1891 (Macmillan) **77** Granger, NYC/Alamy **78** Photo Tristram Brelstaff **82**, **83** from Karl Gjellerup, *Den ældre Eddas Gudesange*, 1895 (Copenhagen) **84** from J. M. Stenersen & Co, *Snorre Sturlason - Heimskringla*, 1899

85 from Wilhelm Wägner, *Nordisch-germanische Götter und Helden*, 1882 (Leipzig) **91** from Vilhelm Grønbech, *Nordiske Myter og Sagn*, 1941 (Copenhagen) **92** from Olive Bray, *Sæmund's Edda*, 1908 (The Viking Club) **94** from Karl Gjellerup, *Den ældre Eddas Gudesange*, 1895 (Copenhagen) **95** from Richard Wagner, *The Rhinegold and the Valkyrie*, 1910 (Quarto) **96** from Rudolf Herzog, *Germaniens Götter*, 1919 (Leipzig) **97** Statens Historiska Museet, Stockholm **99** Árni Magnússon Institute for Icelandic Studies, Reykjavík **100** from Karl Gjellerup, *Den ældre Eddas Gudesange*, 1895 (Copenhagen) **101** Árni Magnússon Institute for Icelandic Studies, Reykjavík **103** Photo Researchers/Alamy **104** DeAgostini/SuperStock **106** Árni Magnússon Institute for Icelandic Studies, Reykjavík **107** from Viktor Rydberg, *Our Fathers' Godsaga*, 1911 (Berlin) **108** British Museum, London **110** from Abbie Farwell Brown, *In the Days of the Giants: A Book of Norse Tales*, 1902 (Houghton, Mifflin and Co.) **114** from Wilhelm Wägner, *Nordisch-germanische Götter und Helden*, 1882 (Leipzig) **115** from Harriet Taylor Treadwell and Margaret Free, *Reading-Literature Fourth Reader*, 1913 (Chicago) **121** from Padraic Colum, *The Children of Odin*, 1920 (Macmillan) **122** Árni Magnússon Institute for Icelandic Studies, Reykjavík **125** from Karl Gjellerup, *Den ældre Eddas Gudesange*, 1895 (Copenhagen) **128** from Martin Oldenbourg, *Walhall, die Götterwelt der Germanen*, 1905 (Berlin) **130** from Padraic Colum, *The Children of Odin*, 1920 (Macmillan) **132** from Felix Dahn, *Walhall: Germanische Götter- und Heldensagen*, 1901 (Breitkopf und Härtel) **133** Richard Wagner Museum, Bayreuth/Dagli Orti/The Art Archive **135** Statens Historiska Museet, Stockholm **137** Granger, NYC/Alamy **138**, **139** Universitetets Oldsaksamling, Oslo/Werner Forman Archive **140** Illustration by Dr Dayanna Knight **141**, **143** Photo Carolyne Larrington **146** from Richard Wagner, *Siegfried & the Twilight of the Gods*, 1911 (London) **148** Universitetets Oldsaksamling, Oslo/Werner Forman Archive **159** from Olaus Magnus, *A Description of the Northern Peoples*, 1555 (Hakluyt Society) **163** from Fredrik Sander, *Poetic Edda*, 1893 (Stockholm) **165** Yolanda Perera Sanchez/Alamy **167** Photo Gilwellian **168** Árni Magnússon Institute for Icelandic Studies, Reykjavík **170** British Museum, London **175** Photo Berig **181** from Olive Bray, *Sæmund's Edda*, 1908 (The Viking Club) **183** Det Kongelige Danske Kunstakademi, Copenhagen **184** Manchester Art Gallery/Bridgeman Images **188** Photo Gerry Millar **190** Nationalmuseum, Stockholm **193** from Olive Bray, *Sæmund's Edda*, 1908 (The Viking Club) **195** from H. A. Guerber, *Myths of the Norsemen from the Eddas and Sagas*, 1909 (London) **196** from Finnur Jónsson, *Goðafræði Norðmanna og Íslendinga eftir heimildum*, 1913 (Reykjavík) **198** from Martin Oldenbourg, *Walhall, die Götterwelt der Germanen*, 1905 (Berlin) **200** Photo Sven Nilsson